NURSING - ISSUES, PROBLEMS AND CHALLENGES

NURSE STAFFING WITHIN THE VETERANS HEALTH ADMINISTRATION

RECRUITMENT, RETENTION AND QUALIFICATION ISSUES

NURSING - ISSUES, PROBLEMS AND CHALLENGES

Additional books in this series can be found on Nova's website under the Series tab.

Additional e-books in this series can be found on Nova's website under the eBooks tab.

NURSING - ISSUES, PROBLEMS AND CHALLENGES

NURSE STAFFING WITHIN THE VETERANS HEALTH ADMINISTRATION

RECRUITMENT, RETENTION AND QUALIFICATION ISSUES

EUGENE GLOVER
EDITOR

New York

Copyright © 2016 by Nova Science Publishers, Inc.

All rights reserved. No part of this book may be reproduced, stored in a retrieval system or transmitted in any form or by any means: electronic, electrostatic, magnetic, tape, mechanical photocopying, recording or otherwise without the written permission of the Publisher.

We have partnered with Copyright Clearance Center to make it easy for you to obtain permissions to reuse content from this publication. Simply navigate to this publication's page on Nova's website and locate the "Get Permission" button below the title description. This button is linked directly to the title's permission page on copyright.com. Alternatively, you can visit copyright.com and search by title, ISBN, or ISSN.

For further questions about using the service on copyright.com, please contact:
Copyright Clearance Center
Phone: +1-(978) 750-8400   Fax: +1-(978) 750-4470   E-mail: info@copyright.com.

NOTICE TO THE READER

The Publisher has taken reasonable care in the preparation of this book, but makes no expressed or implied warranty of any kind and assumes no responsibility for any errors or omissions. No liability is assumed for incidental or consequential damages in connection with or arising out of information contained in this book. The Publisher shall not be liable for any special, consequential, or exemplary damages resulting, in whole or in part, from the readers' use of, or reliance upon, this material. Any parts of this book based on government reports are so indicated and copyright is claimed for those parts to the extent applicable to compilations of such works.

Independent verification should be sought for any data, advice or recommendations contained in this book. In addition, no responsibility is assumed by the publisher for any injury and/or damage to persons or property arising from any methods, products, instructions, ideas or otherwise contained in this publication.

This publication is designed to provide accurate and authoritative information with regard to the subject matter covered herein. It is sold with the clear understanding that the Publisher is not engaged in rendering legal or any other professional services. If legal or any other expert assistance is required, the services of a competent person should be sought. FROM A DECLARATION OF PARTICIPANTS JOINTLY ADOPTED BY A COMMITTEE OF THE AMERICAN BAR ASSOCIATION AND A COMMITTEE OF PUBLISHERS.

Additional color graphics may be available in the e-book version of this book.

Library of Congress Cataloging-in-Publication Data

ISBN: 978-1-63485-264-7

Published by Nova Science Publishers, Inc. † New York

CONTENTS

Preface		vii
Chapter 1	VA Health Care: Oversight Improvements Needed for Nurse Recruitment and Retention Initiatives *United States Government Accountability Office*	1
Chapter 2	VA Health Care: Actions Needed to Ensure Adequate and Qualified Nurse Staffing *United States Government Accountability Office*	31
Index		65

PREFACE

The United States Government Accountability Office (GAO) and others have highlighted the need for an adequate and qualified nurse workforce to provide quality and timely care to veterans. The Department of Veterans Affairs' (VA) Veterans Health Administration (VHA) faces challenges such as increased competition for skilled clinicians in hard-to-fill occupations such as nurses. As GAO has previously reported, recruitment and retention is particularly difficult for nurses with advanced professional skills, knowledge, and experience, which is critical given veterans' needs for more complex specialized services. This book reviews the initiatives VHA has to recruit and retain its nurse workforce and the extent to which VHA oversees its nurse recruitment and retention initiatives. Furthermore, the book reviews the extent to which Department of Veterans Affairs medical centers (VAMC) have implemented VHA's nurse staffing methodology, and VHA oversees VAMCs' implementation and ongoing administration of the methodology.

In: Nurse Staffing Within the Veterans Health ... ISBN: 978-1-63485-264-7
Editor: Eugene Glover © 2016 Nova Science Publishers, Inc.

Chapter 1

VA HEALTH CARE: OVERSIGHT IMPROVEMENTS NEEDED FOR NURSE RECRUITMENT AND RETENTION INITIATIVES[*]

United States Government Accountability Office

WHY GAO DID THIS STUDY

GAO and others have highlighted the need for an adequate and qualified nurse workforce to provide quality and timely care to veterans. VHA faces challenges such as increased competition for skilled clinicians in hard-to-fill occupations such as nurses. As GAO has previously reported, recruitment and retention is particularly difficult for nurses with advanced professional skills, knowledge, and experience, which is critical given veterans' needs for more complex specialized services.

GAO was asked to provide information on the recruitment and retention of nurses within VHA. This report reviews (1) the initiatives VHA has to recruit and retain its nurse workforce and (2) the extent to which VHA oversees its nurse recruitment and retention initiatives. GAO reviewed documents and interviewed officials from VHA, four VA medical centers selected to reflect variation in factors such as nurse turnover, and regional

---

[*] This is an edited, reformatted and augmented version of a United States Government Accountability Office, Publication No. GAO-15-794, dated September 2015.

offices for these medical centers. GAO used federal internal control standards to evaluate VHA's oversight. GAO also interviewed selected stakeholder organizations.

WHAT GAO RECOMMENDS

GAO recommends VA (1) develop a process to help monitor medical centers' compliance with its key nurse recruitment and retention initiatives; (2) evaluate the adequacy of training resources provided to nurse recruiters; and (3) conduct a system-wide evaluation of its key nurse recruitment and retention initiatives. VA concurred with the recommendations.

WHAT GAO FOUND

The Department of Veterans Affairs' (VA) Veterans Health Administration (VHA) has multiple system-wide initiatives to recruit and retain its nurse workforce, but three of the four VA medical centers in GAO's review faced challenges offering them. VHA identified a number of key initiatives it offers to help medical centers recruit and retain nurses, which focus primarily on providing (1) education and training, and (2) financial benefits and incentives. VA medical centers generally have discretion in offering these initiatives. The four medical centers in GAO's review varied in the number of initiatives they offered, and three of these medical centers developed local recruitment and retention initiatives in addition to those offered by VHA. GAO also found that while three of the four medical centers reported improvements in their ability to recruit and retain nurses through their offering of VHA's initiatives; they also reported challenges. The challenges included a lack of sufficient administrative support for medical centers, competition with private sector medical facilities, reduced pool of nurses in rural locations with advanced training, and employee dissatisfaction.

VHA's oversight of its key system-wide nurse recruitment and retention initiatives is limited. Specifically, GAO found that VHA conducts limited monitoring of medical centers' compliance with its initiatives. For example, in the past, VHA conducted site visits in response to a medical center reporting difficulty with implementation of one of its initiatives, and to assess compliance with program policies, but it is no longer conducting these visits.

Consistent with federal internal control standards, monitoring should be ongoing and should identify performance gaps in a policy or procedure. With limited monitoring, VHA lacks assurance that its medical centers are complying with its nurse recruitment and retention initiatives, and that any problems are identified and resolved in a timely and appropriate manner. In addition, VHA has not conducted evaluations of the training resources provided to nurse recruiters at VA medical centers or the overall effectiveness of the initiatives in meeting its nurse recruitment and retention goals, or whether any changes are needed. Consistent with federal internal control standards, measuring performance tracks progress towards program goals and objectives, and provides important information to make management decisions and resolve any problems or program weaknesses. For example, GAO found that VHA does not know whether medical centers have sufficient training to support its nurse recruitment and retention initiatives. In particular, there is currently no face-to-face training provided by VHA specifically for nurse recruiters, but there is regular training available to those assigned to a human resources office as part of training available to all human resources staff. Representatives from a national nursing organization reported that clinical nurse recruiters at VA medical centers often feel more unprepared for the position than those assigned to human resources offices, but no evaluation of this disparity or its effects has occurred. Without evaluations of its collective system-wide initiatives, VHA is unable to determine to what extent its nurse recruitment and retention initiatives are effective in meeting VHA policies and the Veterans Access, Choice, and Accountability Act provisions, or ultimately whether VHA has an adequate and qualified nurse workforce at its medical centers that is sufficient to meet veterans' health care needs.

ABBREVIATIONS

Choice Act	Veterans Access, Choice, and Accountability Act of 2014
FY	fiscal year
GPRA	Government Performance and Results Act of 1993
LPN	licensed practical nurse
NA	nursing assistant
NP	nurse practitioner
OIG	Office of Inspector General
RN	registered nurse
VA	Department of Veterans Affairs

VHA	Veterans Health Administration
VISN	Veterans Integrated Service Network

* * *

September 30, 2015
The Honorable Mike Coffman
Chairman
Subcommittee on Oversight & Investigations
Committee on Veterans' Affairs
House of Representatives
Dear Mr. Chairman:

The Department of Veterans Affairs' (VA) Veterans Health Administration's (VHA) mission is to provide quality and timely care for veterans. It is essential that VHA recruit and retain an adequate number of skilled clinicians, including nurses, at its 167 medical centers across the country to achieve its mission. VHA faces difficulties ensuring it has the appropriate clinical workforce to meet the current and future needs of veterans due to factors such as national shortages and increased competition for clinicians in hard-to-fill occupations, including nurses. We previously reported that VHA noted particular difficulty recruiting and retaining nurses with advanced professional skills, knowledge, and experience, which are particularly important for certain hospital units, such as intensive care units, that require higher-intensity nursing.[1] In spite of an increase in the number of students enrolled in nurse programs throughout the U.S., some areas of the country are expected to experience a smaller growth in nurses, and demand for nurses with the advanced education needed to provide more highly skilled patient care will likely persist.[2]

Recent events have further highlighted the need for adequate and qualified clinicians to provide quality and timely care to veterans. In 2014, GAO, VA's Office of Inspector General (OIG), and other stakeholders testified before Congress on patient deaths alleged to be related to delays in patient care, long patient wait times, and problematic scheduling practices at VA medical centers. Some of the stakeholders concluded that VHA needed additional clinical staff, including nurses, to provide quality care to veterans in a timely manner. In addition, Congress passed the Veterans Access, Choice, and Accountability Act of 2014 (Choice Act), which appropriated $5 billion to, among other things, hire additional clinical staff, including nurses.[3] VHA reported that more than 10,000 additional clinicians and support staff will be hired by the end of fiscal year (FY) 2016 to help meet the needs of VA medical centers across the country. In January 2015, the VA OIG reported on the five VHA occupations with the highest staffing shortages; nursing was second among those occupations.[4]

You asked for information on nurse recruitment and retention at VA medical centers. In this report, we reviewed (1) key initiatives VHA has to recruit and retain its nurse workforce and (2) the extent to which VHA oversees its nurse recruitment and retention initiatives.

To identify key initiatives VHA has to recruit and retain its nurse workforce, we reviewed VHA documents and reports describing its system-wide recruitment and retention initiatives for nurses. We identified as key those initiatives with primary goals that included the recruitment and retention of nurses. We reviewed policies and procedures that guide VA medical centers in offering these initiatives to nurses, and reviewed documentation of annual assessments and program evaluations to identify any potential successes or difficulties in recruiting and retaining nurses, generally, or by specialty or position type—nurse practitioners (NP), registered nurses (RN), licensed practical nurses (LPN), or nursing assistants (NA). (Unless otherwise noted, the term "nurses" in this report includes all position types.) We interviewed officials from VHA's central office—Office of Nursing Services, Office of Academic Affiliations, Healthcare Talent Management, and Workforce Management & Consulting—about the key system-wide initiatives they have to help VA medical centers recruit and retain nurses. We also reviewed VHA data, such as funding levels for the initiatives, the number of VA medical centers offering the initiatives, and the number of nurses that participated, from FY 2010 through FY 2014.[5] We assessed the reliability of these data through reviews of supporting documentation and interviews with knowledgeable VHA officials and determined that they were sufficiently reliable for our purposes.

In addition, we reviewed documents and interviewed officials and nursing staff from four VA medical centers located in (1) Iron Mountain, Michigan; (2) Oklahoma City, Oklahoma; (3) San Francisco, California; and (4) Wilmington, Delaware about the extent to which they offered VHA's key recruitment and retention initiatives to nurses from FY 2010 through FY 2014 and their experiences doing so, as well as any initiatives developed locally—at each medical center or its respective Veterans Integrated Service Network (VISN).[6] In particular, we interviewed medical center officials about any successes or difficulties in offering VHA and any local initiatives to nurses, any improvements needed to the initiatives, and the effectiveness of the initiatives in recruiting and retaining nurses at their medical center. We selected the four medical centers to reflect variation in factors such as average nurse turnover rate, geographic location, rural vs. urban location, and facility complexity.[7] For each of the four medical centers, we reviewed documents describing any recruitment and retention initiatives developed by the medical center or its associated VISN, as well as any local policies and procedures used to guide the medical center in offering VHA and local initiatives. We also interviewed officials from the VISNs associated with these four VA medical centers. We did not collect information on local initiatives at all VA medical centers; therefore, this information is not generalizable system-wide. We also interviewed representatives of veterans service organizations, nursing organizations, and unions that represent nurses at the selected medical centers about the recruitment and retention of nurses, including the extent to which VHA initiatives have improved the recruitment and retention of nurses at VA medical centers.[8]

To determine the extent to which VHA oversees its key recruitment and retention initiatives for nurses, we reviewed documents, such as VHA directives, policies, and evaluation plans that describe requirements and guidance regarding VHA's and VISNs' oversight of the initiatives. We interviewed officials from VHA and the VISNs associated with the four VA medical centers included in our review regarding their oversight, including the extent to which VHA evaluates the effectiveness of the initiatives; monitors medical center compliance with the policies related to VHA's recruitment and retention initiatives; provides clear and comprehensive communication to medical centers; and collects, assesses, and incorporates feedback to improve the initiatives. We reviewed documents, such as any local policies or evaluations, and conducted interviews with officials from the VA medical centers about the oversight they conduct at each of their respective medical centers. We determined whether VHA applied appropriate internal controls in its oversight of the key recruitment and retention initiatives for nurses by reviewing relevant criteria from federal internal control standards.[9] We also reviewed relevant criteria from GAO's body of work on effectively managing performance under the Government Performance and Results Act of 1993 (GPRA), as enhanced by the GPRA Modernization Act of 2010.[10]

We conducted this performance audit from October 2014 through September 2015 in accordance with generally accepted government auditing standards. Those standards require that we plan and perform the audit to obtain sufficient, appropriate evidence to provide a reasonable basis for our findings and conclusions based on our audit objectives. We believe that the evidence obtained provides a reasonable basis for our findings and conclusions based on our audit objectives.

BACKGROUND

Nurse recruitment and retention is essential for VHA to carry out its mission to provide quality care that improves the health and well-being of veterans. In its 2014 Interim Workforce and Succession Strategic Plan, VHA identified nurses as the second most mission-critical occupation for recruitment and retention; only physicians ranked higher.[11] As the demand for health care services increases, effective nurse recruitment and retention is increasingly important for VHA to ensure an adequate and qualified workforce.

VHA's Nurse Workforce

In the last 5 years, the number of nurses providing care to veterans has increased, and VHA expects it will continue to increase because of the expected increased demand for services. In FY 2014, VHA employed more than 85,000 nurses who provided both direct and indirect care to patients through its health care system.[12] The number of nurses providing direct patient care has increased from about 72,000 to about 82,000—approximately a 14 percent increase—from FY 2010 through FY 2014, while the number of unique patients served increased from about 6.0 million to about 6.6 million—approximately a 10 percent increase—during this same time period. VHA projects that approximately 40,000 new RNs will be needed through FY 2018 to maintain adequate staffing levels, including replacing retired nurses, to meet veterans' needs. (See app. I for the number of nurses providing direct and indirect care at VA medical centers from FY 2010 through FY 2014.)

In addition to the need for more nurses due to an increasing number of veterans, VHA anticipates that changes in veteran demographics, including an aging population, will increase the need for nurses to provide more complex types of services to care for veterans. In its 2014 Interim Workforce and Succession Strategic Plan, VHA reported that after 2015, the largest segment of the veteran population will be between 65 and 84 years of age. Also, the number of women veterans receiving care through VHA has nearly doubled since 2004, requiring changes to the type of care provided and corresponding skills needed. VHA estimates that veteran usage of primary care, surgical specialty care, and mental health care will each increase by more than 20 percent over the next 10 years.

VHA Nurse Skill Mix

The nurse skill mix—the proportion of each type of nurse (NPs, RNs, LPNs, and NAs) of the total nursing staff in a particular unit or medical center—is an important component of VHA nurse staffing, as the level of education and training for each nurse position determines the types of services that can be provided.[13] (See table 1 for VHA nurse positions, responsibilities, and educational requirements.) For example, intensive care units require higher intensity nursing, and may have a skill mix that is primarily composed of RNs compared to other types of units that may provide less complex care, such as outpatient clinics.

Table 1. Veterans Health Administration (VHA) Nurse Positions, Responsibilities, and Educational Requirements

Position type	Responsibilities	Educational requirements
Nurse practitioner (NP)	Independently assesses and evaluates patients, provides care, administers medications, documents patients' medical conditions including admissions and discharges, analyzes test results, establishes treatment plans, and operates medical equipment.[a]	Completed an advanced nursing education program, met state licensing requirements, and maintains a current certification to obtain an NP license.
Registered nurse (RN)	Provides care to patients, administers medications, documents patients' medical conditions including admissions and discharges, analyzes test results, establishes treatment plans, and operates medical equipment.	Completed a nursing education program, met state licensing requirements, and passed a nurse licensing examination to obtain an RN license.

Position type	Responsibilities	Educational requirements
Licensed practical nurse (LPN)	Takes patient vital signs, provides basic care, and administers medications, but generally does not provide certain complex patient care services such as patient assessments or administration of intravenous medications.	Obtained a high school diploma or its equivalent and passed a licensing examination upon completion of a state-approved program available at technical schoolsand community colleges, typically lasting 1 year.
Nursing assistant (NA)	Attends to basic patient needs such as providing personal care to patients (e.g., assistance with bathing, dressing, and hygiene), carries out non-specialized duties (e.g., measures blood pressure), and supports other nursing staff.	Registered as a nursing assistant with relevant state health department, and passed a written competency examination upon completion of a state-approved training program, generally lasting 3 to 12 weeks.

Source: VHA. I GAO-15-794

Note: Under statutory authority, VA establishes the educational requirements of its health care practitioners, including NPs, RNs, LPNs, and NAs.

[a]NP scope of practice is determined by the individual medical center and/or relevant state.

In the last 5 fiscal years, RNs comprised the largest percentage of nurses within VHA, and were approximately 64 percent of the nurse workforce in FY 2014. NPs comprised the smallest percentage over the same period. (See figure 1.)

For the first time, in FY 2015, VA began collecting data on the number of nurse hires and vacancies at each of its medical centers. For FY 2015, as of June, VA medical centers hired approximately 8,600 nurses; approximately 5,100 (59 percent) were RNs, and approximately 430 were NPs (5 percent), reflecting VHA's need for nurses with advanced skills and education. Despite these new hires, VHA estimated that there were about 17,000 vacancies across VA medical centers as of June 2015, with about 12,100 (71 percent) for RN positions. (See app. I for the number of nurse hires and losses at VA medical centers for FY 2015, as of June.)

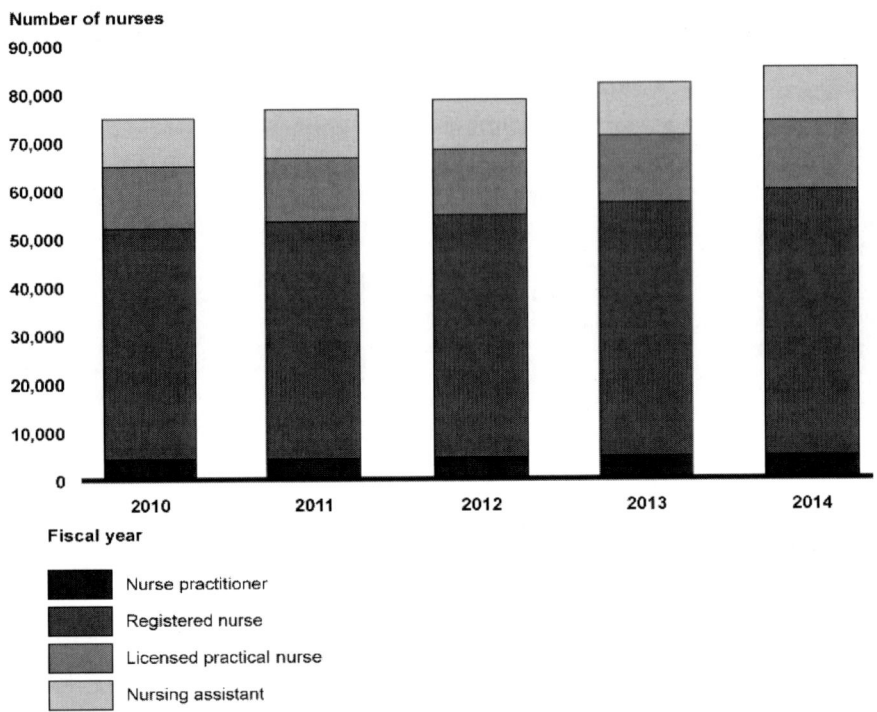

Source: VHA. | GAO-15-794

Note: The figure reflects the overall VHA nurse workforce, including nurses providing direct and indirect care services.

Figure 1. Skill Mix of the Veterans Health Administration's (VHA) Nurse Workforce at VA Medical Centers by Position Type, Fiscal Year (FY) 2010 through FY 2014.

The average national nurse turnover rate for VHA from FY 2010 through FY 2014 was 7.6 percent.[14] The turnover rates for NPs and RNs increased over this same period, and in FY 2014, were 9.1 percent and 7.8 percent, respectively. VHA reported high projected losses for nurses, such as from retirement, in the next few fiscal years. In 2014, for example, VHA reported that by FY 2019, approximately 20 percent of its nurses will be eligible for retirement. Retirement and career advancement through opportunities elsewhere were the top two reasons why nurses reportedly left VHA. In addition, according to findings from VHA's 2015 Workforce Planning Report, approximately 12 percent of all nurses that left VHA in FY 2012 did so in their first year of employment. (See app I. for annual nurse turnover rates by position type for FY 2010 through FY 2014.)

Roles and Responsibilities for VHA Nurse Recruitment and Retention

VA medical centers are responsible for recruiting and retaining nurses in their respective facilities, with VHA providing support to assist them. Specifically, VHA has developed initiatives that medical centers may offer to help with the recruitment and retention of nurses. VHA also provides guidance and policies to its medical centers on the process of recruiting and hiring nurses and on the initiatives medical centers may use to help with recruitment and retention. Additionally, VHA provides marketing services and tools to medical centers, including marketing campaigns that advertise the benefits of working at VHA and recruitment brochures that medical centers can use at local career fairs. Nurse recruitment begins with advertising and publicizing available positions to encourage potential candidates to apply, through various channels, including through local publications, job fairs, and USAjobs.gov.[15] Once medical centers recruit, interview, and select a nursing candidate, that nursing candidate goes through a process known as onboarding and credentialing.[16]

Most medical centers employ nurse recruiters, who are responsible for managing the administrative components of the hiring process, as well as various aspects of nurse recruitment and retention. The nurse recruiter position varies among medical centers. Some medical centers assign the nurse recruiter to the medical center's clinical nursing services office, and these nurse recruiters are typically RNs. Other medical centers assign nurse recruiters to the medical center's human resources office, and these nurse recruiters may not have clinical backgrounds.

VHA HAS MULTIPLE NURSE RECRUITMENT AND RETENTION INITIATIVES, BUT SOME MEDICAL CENTERS FACE CHALLENGES THAT LIMIT THE INITIATIVES' USEFULNESS

VHA has multiple system-wide initiatives to recruit and retain its nurse workforce, but some VA medical centers face challenges in offering them to nurses and with recruitment and retention more broadly. We found that VHA has eight key initiatives that medical centers may offer to help them recruit and retain nurses. (See table 2.) VHA's initiatives focus primarily on providing (1) education and training, and (2) financial benefits and incentives.[17] (See app. II for VHA expenditures for and nurse participation in key recruitment and retention initiatives from FY 2010 through FY 2014.)

Table 2. Veterans Health Administration's (VHA) Key Nurse Recruitment and Retention Initiatives, as of July 2015

Initiative	Description
Education and training initiatives	
RN Transition to Practice	Provides 12-month standardized on-the-job training to assist registered nurses (RN) with 1 year or less of nursing experience with their transition from entry-level to professional nurse. All VA medical centers that hire RNs with 1 year or less of experience are required to offer this initiative.
VA Learning Opportunities Residency	Provides eligible nursing students who have completed their junior years of accredited nursing programs with hands-on learning opportunities through full- or part-time summer employment at VA medical centers.a VA medical centers must submit requests for proposals, and VHA funds selected medical centers for 5 years.
VA Nursing Academic Partnerships	Provides funding for partnerships between VA medical centers and schools of nursing for baccalaureate degree programs. The partnerships are to provide veteran-centric initiatives and opportunities for clinical education at VA medical centers. Schools of nursing agree to increase student enrollment by a certain number of students for each VA nurse who serves as a faculty member. VA medical centers must submit requests for proposals, and VHA funds selected medical centers for 5 years. Funds are intended to assist medical centers in developing residency programs for undergraduate students in collaboration with schools of nursing and to assist with hiring faculty and program directors at both medical centers and schools of nursing. Selected VA medical centers must also offer a Post-Baccalaureate Nurse Residency, which has a defined curriculum based on national accreditation standards and clinical requirements for RNs graduating from a baccalaureate degree program.b

Initiative	Description
VA Nursing Academic Partnerships – Graduate Education	Provides funding for partnerships between VA medical centers and schools of nursing for graduate education programs. The partnerships are to provide veteran-centric initiatives and opportunities for clinical education at VA medical centers. Schools of nursing agree to increase student enrollment by a certain number of students for each VA nurse who serves as a faculty member. VA medical centers must submit requests for proposals, and VHA funds selected medical centers for 5 years. Funds are intended to assist medical centers in developing residency programs for graduate students in collaboration with schools of nursing and to assistwith hiring faculty and program directors at both medical centers and schools of nursing. Selected VA medical centers are expected to offer one or more of the following residency programs: Acute Care Nurse Practitioner Residency, Adult-Gerontology Nurse Practitioner Residency, or Psychiatric Mental Health Nurse Practitioner Residency.c
Financial benefits and incentives initiatives	
Recruitment, retention, and relocation incentives	Provides financial incentives for prospective or current VA employees, including nurses, in hard-to-recruit or hard-to-retain positions.
EducationDebt Reduction Program	Reimburses qualifying education loan debt for staff, including nurses, in hard-to-recruit positions. Nurses apply directly to the medical center, and applications are approved by VHA. The Veterans Access, Choice, and Accountability Act of 2014 increased the maximum reimbursement per recipient from $60,000 to $120,000. VHA reimburses nurses up to $120,000 for 5-year service period.
Employee Incentive Scholarship Program	Provides scholarships to healthcare professionals, including nurses, pursuing associate, baccalaureate, and advanced degree programs, and replacement salaries to VA medical centers with scholarship recipients attending school full time.Nurses apply directly to the medical center, and applications are approved by VHA. Nurses may receive funds for the equivalent of a 3-year full-time degree program. After completing the degree program, nurses must also enter into a service obligation, ranging from 1 to 3 years, as a full-time employee.

Table 2. (Continued)

Initiative	Description
	Components of this initiative include the National Nursing Education Initiative, which provides scholarships to RNs, and the VA National Education for Employees Program, which reimburses medical centers for salaries of scholarship recipients who are attending school full time.
Flexible work schedules	Allows variations in nurse work schedules, such as different shifts, the number of days worked per pay period, and options to work part-time schedules.

Source: VHA. | GAO-15-794

Notes: Unless otherwise indicated, VA medical centers had discretion in offering VHA's recruitment and retention initiatives for nurses.

VHA has other initiatives that may aid in the recruitment and retention of nurses, such as special advancements for performance or nursing achievements. For the purposes of this report, we focused on VHA's initiatives whose primary goals included nurse recruitment and retention.

[a] RNs who were former VA Learning Opportunities Residency students were eligible to be hired at VA medical centers at higher salaries based on their performance in the residency, or the number of hours they completed as residents.

[b] In 2011, VHA introduced the Post-Baccalaureate Nurse Residency as a stand-alone initiative. In 2015, VHA rolled the residency into the existing VA Nursing Academic Partnerships initiative for new applicants to begin in academic year 2015-2016. RNs who complete the Post-Baccalaureate Nurse Residency are eligible to be hired at VA medical centers at higher salaries.

[c] In 2013, VHA introduced the Psychiatric Mental Health Nurse Practitioner Residency as a standalone initiative. In 2015, VHA introduced a graduate-education initiative—the VA Nursing Academic Partnerships – Graduate Education—into which it rolled the residency for new applicants.

With the exception of the mandatory RN Transition to Practice initiative, VA medical centers generally have discretion to offer any of VHA's initiatives to nurses, including the discretion to submit requests for proposals for any of the initiatives that require them. The four VA medical centers in our review varied in the number of initiatives they offered from FY 2010 through FY 2014. (See table 3.) For example, one of the medical centers in our review offered three of the four education and training initiatives—RN Transition to Practice, VA Nursing Academic Partnerships, and VA Learning Opportunities Residency. This medical center also offered the Post-Baccalaureate Nurse Residency—which, beginning in FY 2015, is part of the VA Nursing

Academic Partnerships—and developed curricula to move participants through the initiatives.[18] This medical center also offered all four of the financial initiatives—recruitment, retention, and relocation incentives; the Education Debt Reduction Program; the Employee Incentive Scholarship Program; and flexible work schedules.[19] The medical center ceased offering recruitment, retention, and relocation incentives in 2013; according to medical center officials, VHA introduced new employee performance criteria that medical center officials felt were too difficult for employees to achieve or for medical centers to provide justification for retention incentives. Officials from all four medical centers reported offering flexible work schedules to provide nurses with options when trying to maintain work life balance, such as offering nurses compressed schedules (e.g., 10-hour shifts, 4 days a week).[20]

While VA medical centers generally have discretion to offer any of VHA's initiatives, all medical centers that employed RNs with less than 1 year of nursing experience were required to offer the RN Transition to Practice initiative.[21] However, officials from two medical centers in our review reported not offering the initiative at all or not offering it across all 5 fiscal years. Officials from one medical center offered the RN Transition to Practice initiative for 1 year, beginning in 2012, but subsequently decided not to hire newly graduated nurses because of the extensive orientation and training they required. According to officials, after one of its current LPNs returned to school to become an RN, this medical center coordinated with another VA medical center in the region for this new RN to participate in that medical center's RN Transition to Practice curriculum. Officials from the second medical center told us that it offered a 16-week program designed to help new nurses acclimate to VA but did not offer VHA's 12-month RN Transition to Practice initiative because they did not believe it was required.

In addition to offering VHA's initiatives, three of the four medical centers in our review developed local recruitment and retention initiatives. Two medical centers developed initiatives to provide employment to train student nurses; the medical centers' initiatives were similar to the VA Learning Opportunities Residency. Officials from one of these medical centers told us that the medical center developed a local initiative because the nursing schools in the region offered associate degrees only; whereas, VHA's initiative requires medical centers to partner with schools of nursing with baccalaureate degree programs. The other medical center offered the VA Learning Opportunities Residency, as well as its own student nurse employment and training initiative. Officials from a third medical center in our review told us that the medical center offered a 16- week RN Transition to Practice initiative to train new RN graduates; these RNs are hired on a temporary basis and are hired as full-time employees when RN vacancies open.

Table 3. Veterans Health Administration's (VHA) Key Nurse Recruitment and Retention Initiatives Offered by Four Selected Medical Centers during Fiscal Years (FY) 2010 through 2014

Initiative	Medical Center A	Medical Center B	Medical Center C	Medical Center D
Education and training initiatives				
RN Transition to Practice	X	X		X
VA Learning Opportunities Residency		X		X
VA Nursing Academic Partnerships[a]		X[b]		
VA Nursing Academic Partnerships – Graduate Education[c]				
Financial benefits and incentives initiatives				
Recruitment, retention, and relocation incentives	X	X	X	
Education Debt Reduction Program	X	X	X	X
Employee Incentive Scholarship Program	X	X	X	X
Flexible work schedules	X	X	X	X

Source: VA medical centers in our review. | GAO-15-794

Note: An "X" in a column indicates that the medical center offered the VHA recruitment and retention initiative to nurses for at least 1 year during the 5-year period.

[a]In 2011, VHA introduced the Post-Baccalaureate Nurse Residency as a stand-alone initiative. In 2015, VHA rolled this residency into the existing VA Nursing Academic Partnerships initiative for new applicants to begin in academic year 2015-2016.

[b]Medical Center B offered the VA Nursing Academic Partnerships during the FY 2010 through FY 2014 period, as well as the Post-Baccalaureate Nurse Residency when it was a stand-alone initiative.

[c]In 2013, VHA introduced the Psychiatric Mental Health Nurse Practitioner Residency as a standalone initiative, and none of the selected medical centers offered this initiative during the period of our review. In 2015, VHA introduced a graduate-education track—the VA Nursing Academic Partnerships – Graduate Education—into which it rolled the residency for new applicants.

Officials from three of the four medical centers in our review reported that VHA's initiatives helped improve their ability to recruit and retain nurses, as shown in the following examples:

- Officials from one medical center reported that they hired 9 of the 10 nurses who participated in the VHA Post-Baccalaureate Nurse Residency as full-time nurses in academic year 2012-2013, the first year the medical center offered the initiative. The medical center retained 7 of these 9 nurses as of the end of the following academic year 2013-2014.
- Officials from another medical center that offered the Education Debt Reduction Program reported that, of the six nurses that began the program since 2010, five completed the 5-year service agreement and, as of April 2015, remained employees of the medical center.
- Officials from one medical center that offered the Employee Incentive Scholarship Program reported that 23 nurses completed the program over the past 10 years, and, as of February 2015, 21 of those nurses have remained employees of the medical center.

Despite these successes, however, officials from three of the four medical centers in our review reported challenges with offering VHA's initiatives specifically, and recruiting and retaining nurses more broadly, both of which limited the initiatives' usefulness. These challenges—lack of sufficient administrative support, competition with private sector medical facilities for qualified and skilled nurses, the rural location of the medical center, and employee dissatisfaction—may affect medical centers' ability to effectively and efficiently recruit and retain nurses.

- **Lack of sufficient administrative support**. Officials from one medical center reported challenges in efficiently offering some of the initiatives due to the lack of sufficient administrative support. Specifically, medical center officials reported not having sufficient human resources and clerical staff to process in a timely manner the paperwork associated with specific VHA recruitment and retention initiatives, such as the Employee Incentive Scholarship Program.
- **Competition with the private sector**. Officials from two medical centers reported challenges in recruiting and retaining nurses because of competition with private hospitals in the area. Officials from one medical center told us that they face significant competition from

local hospitals, as there are multiple private boutique and specialty hospitals in their area. Officials stated that competing with these hospitals, especially for entry-level nurses, is difficult because the hospitals offer generous signing bonuses. Officials from another medical center told us that the high cost of living and lower nursing salaries compared to the salaries offered by competing medical facilities in the area negatively affects the medical center's ability to successfully recruit and retain nurses, specifically RNs and NPs. Officials from this medical center told us that they do not have sufficient funds, such as funds from VHA's Education Debt Reduction Program, to offer nurses financial incentives to make up for the large difference in salaries. In addition, while the Choice Act increased the maximum repayment amount for each recipient of the Education Debt Reduction Program from $60,000 to $120,000, VHA officials told us that VHA did not increase the medical center's annual funding allocation for the program to account for that increase.[22] In FY 2014, this medical center had turnover rates of 10 percent or higher for NPs, RNs, and LPNs, above the national average of 7.9 percent for all nurses.

- **Rural location**. Officials from one medical center that has community outpatient clinics located in rural areas reported challenges recruiting qualified nurses with the requisite experience to work in critical care or other specialized units such as mental health. Officials from another medical center located in a rural area reported that, while the medical center receives high interest in nurse employment generally from the community and has a ready applicant pool for some nurses, it also faces challenges in recruiting nurses with advanced degrees or advanced training and expertise to work in the emergency department or intensive care unit because of its rural location.

- **Employee dissatisfaction**. Officials from one medical center and its union reported high levels of nurse dissatisfaction with medical center leadership as a result of recent investigations, including by VA's OIG, examining access to care issues in the facility. This dissatisfaction has negatively affected the medical center's ability to retain nurses, according to officials from this medical center. In FY 2014, for example, this medical center had a 12 percent turnover rate for NPs and close to a 30 percent turnover rate for NAs. With some nurses on administrative leave and high nurse turnover, officials stated that nurses are stepping into positions temporarily and are being asked to work additional or longer shifts. Officials stated that the medical center's units are inadequately staffed to care for the medical center's current patient load, which they believe is affecting access and the quality of care provided to veterans.

In addition to challenges identified by the medical centers in our review, VHA also identified a challenge specific to the RN Transition to Practice initiative. Officials from the Office of Nursing Services told us that, when VHA began to require medical centers to offer the RN Transition to Practice initiative in November 2011, VHA did not provide specific funding to medical centers to do so and relied on medical centers to determine how to fund the initiative, which is financially and staff-resource intensive. According to VHA officials, there have been two unintended consequences of requiring medical centers to offer this initiative without VHA funding. First, some medical centers are deciding to hire experienced RNs only, who would not be eligible for the initiative, rather than hiring new RNs because of the financial burden associated with the initiative. Second, some medical centers in rural locations have found it difficult to offer the initiative because of a lack of available instructors qualified to provide the required training.

VHA's Oversight of Its Nurse Recruitment and Retention Initiatives Is Limited

VHA Conducts Limited Monitoring of VA Medical Centers' Compliance with Nurse Recruitment and Retention Initiatives

VHA conducts limited monitoring of VA medical centers to ensure they are in compliance with its key nurse recruitment and retention initiatives. Consistent with federal internal control standards, monitoring should be ongoing in the course of normal program operations and provide reasonable assurance of compliance with applicable laws and regulations.[23] VHA's Office of Academic Affiliations has a system in place for conducting site visits to the medical centers that offer the VA Nursing Academic Partnerships initiative. Office of Academic Affiliations officials reported that the site visits occur at least once per year to gauge a medical center's adherence to the residency's policies and contractual requirements. In addition to providing consulting services during these site visits to all medical centers that offer this initiative, these officials also told us that site visit reports are specifically generated for medical centers that are offering the initiative for the first time, and these reports are provided to the nursing school and medical center leadership. Officials told us that they have stopped three medical centers from offering the VA Nursing Academic Partnerships initiative when it was in the pilot phase due to non-compliance with program policies.

VHA Healthcare Talent Management officials told us that although they conducted site visits to medical centers in the past that offered the Education Debt Reduction Program, they are currently not conducting site visits. Officials reported that these site visits were in response to a medical center reporting difficulty implementing the initiatives the office manages, and were a method of comprehensively assessing individual medical center's compliance with policies or guidance, as well as being consultative in nature. A Healthcare Talent Management official reported that the office lacked sufficient staff to enable them to conduct any site visits in FY 2015 and that additional staff have been hired, which will enable the office to resume site visits in FY 2016.

In addition, although VHA required VA medical centers, as of November 2011, to offer VHA's RN Transition to Practice initiative to RNs with 1 year or less of experience, the Office of Nursing Services does not have a process in place to determine if all medical centers are in compliance. We found, for example, that one medical center in our review that employed RNs with less than 1 year of experience had not offered the RN Transition to Practice initiative; officials from this medical center stated that they thought the initiative was recommended and not required. Officials from the Office of Nursing Services told us that, when the RN Transition to Practice initiative became a requirement in November 2011, there was no specific funding provided to medical centers to offer it. Because of this lack of funding, officials said that it has been difficult to provide oversight of this initiative. With limited monitoring taking place as part of its oversight, VHA lacks assurance that its medical centers are complying with the recruitment and retention initiatives' policies and requirements, and that any problems can be identified and resolved in a timely and appropriate manner.

VHA Has Conducted Limited Evaluations of the Training Resources Provided and Overall Nurse Recruitment and Retention Initiatives

Although three VA medical centers in our review reported that VHA's key recruitment and retention initiatives for nurses have been helpful, VHA has conducted limited evaluations to determine any needed training resources or to determine the initiatives' effectiveness system-wide and whether any changes are needed. This lack of evaluation may affect VHA's ability to improve the initiatives and ultimately medical centers' ability to recruit and retain nurses. Consistent with federal internal control standards, measuring performance allows organizations to track the progress they are making towards program goals and objectives, and provides managers important information on which to make management decisions and resolve any problems or program weaknesses.[24]

According to VHA officials, there are processes in place to determine if problems exist with several of its recruitment and retention initiatives. First, for the first time, in FY 2015, VHA's Healthcare Talent Management conducted a survey of medical centers as part of the data collection process for VHA's Interim Workforce and Succession Strategic Plan.[25]

The purpose of the survey was to collect information on workforce priorities in the field and to gauge barriers to medical centers as they offer the three recruitment and retention initiatives managed by Healthcare Talent Management.[26] The survey responses provided feedback on some of the barriers that medical centers faced with offering the initiatives, such as an application process for the Education Debt Reduction Program that was not user friendly. Healthcare Talent Management officials said they plan to use these survey results to make changes to the initiatives it manages, and the office plans to continue including questions regarding workforce planning priorities in future surveys.

Second, VHA's Office of Nursing Services is currently conducting a formal evaluation of the RN Transition to Practice initiative. According to an official, the purpose of the evaluation is to gather information on any successes that medical centers have experienced with offering the initiative. As part of the data collection process, the evaluation team has started interviewing program coordinators at selected medical centers, and will analyze available participant survey data. In addition, the evaluation team plans to survey all medical centers to gauge their compliance with the requirement that all medical centers with RNs with 1 year or less of experience offer the initiative. According to officials, the initiative is set to expire in 2016, and VHA will use the information from the evaluation to make decisions and set goals regarding the program moving forward.

Lastly, the Office of Academic Affiliations uses various tools to assess nurse residents' skill competency and satisfaction with the initiatives it manages. For example, it uses an assessment tool to measure nurses' progress toward the development of core clinical competencies at set intervals throughout their participation in the VA Nursing Academic Partnerships, specifically the Post-Baccalaureate Nurse Residency. The Office of Academic Affiliations also uses a survey to gauge participating students' satisfaction with its training programs and residencies, including the VA Nursing Academic Partnerships - Graduate Education initiative, on topics such as the learning and working environments, as well as clinical faculty skills.

However, VHA has not conducted any assessments of the adequacy of training resources for nurse recruiters. In particular, there are substantial differences in the availability of training resources for nurse recruiters, who can play a key role in medical centers offering VHA's nurse recruitment and retention initiatives to nurses, according to officials from VHA and representatives of a national nursing organization. According to a VHA official, there is currently no face-to-face training provided by VHA specifically for nurse recruiters, but there is regular training available to those assigned to a human resources office as part of training available to all human resources staff. Representatives of a national nursing organization reported that the clinical nurse recruiters at VA medical centers often feel overwhelmed and unprepared in the position because of a lack of training and human resources-related information, which may have resulted in turnover in that position. VHA officials told us that these differences in training for different types of nurse recruiters have existed for years, but no review of the training provided to nurse recruiters has been conducted. Further, VHA officials told us there are no current plans to assess the differences in the training and the effect that it has on the effectiveness of nurse recruiters. VHA officials reported that the barrier to conducting this type of assessment was resources, both a lack of funding, as well as a lack of staff to conduct the assessment.

Furthermore, VHA has not conducted any evaluations of the overall effectiveness of the key initiatives in meeting VHA's system-wide nurse recruitment and retention goals. In its 2014 Interim Workforce and Succession Strategic Plan, VHA reported that its plan included recruiting highly skilled employees in mission critical occupations, which includes nurses, who are able to function at the top of the competency level, as well as retaining these employees as VHA develops a pipeline of qualified nurses that will take on more senior roles.[27] In addition, VHA reported that it is challenged with ensuring it has the appropriate workforce to meet current and future needs that result from shortages and competition for certain health care positions, such as nurses. For example, 42 percent of VHA's senior leadership, which includes senior-level nurses, is eligible for retirement in 2015, and this percentage will increase over the next 7 years. The strategic plan noted that VHA has several initiatives, such as the Education Debt Reduction Program, to address some of its recruitment challenges, but does not discuss the effectiveness of this initiative in meeting recruitment goals. VA's annual report to Congress presents statistical information on some of VHA's recruitment and retention initiatives, such as the number of nurses that received financial incentives in FY 2014 and the amount of financial incentives paid during that time, but does not provide information on the effectiveness of those initiatives in the recruitment and retention of nurses.[28]

VHA officials reported that they hold regular and ad hoc meetings for all offices that manage VHA's nurse recruitment and retention initiatives to discuss a variety of topics, such as coordination and effectiveness. For example, the Office of Academic Affiliations holds ad hoc meetings with the Office of Nursing Services and Healthcare Talent Management to coordinate their initiatives related to recruitment and retention. In addition, Healthcare Talent Management holds quarterly meetings with the Office of Academic Affiliations and the Office of Nursing Services to share data, coordinate resources, and offer support for the other offices' programs. Although these offices may meet to discuss the management of the initiatives, VHA officials reported no current plans to evaluate the overall effectiveness of the initiatives in meeting strategic goals.

A VHA official noted that the lack of evaluations of the overall effectiveness of VHA's initiatives is a gap in the organization's oversight. This official said that the recruitment and retention initiatives for nurses are offered at the local medical center level, and their role has primarily been to provide consultative services to those facilities. VHA officials noted that some data are regularly maintained at the national level, and although they are able to gather limited data on the initiatives from the medical centers, they need to develop a process to evaluate its initiatives to provide better support.

Oversight that includes evaluations of individual initiatives, if conducted, could provide VHA with data to identify any resource needs, such as training or administrative needs, and difficulties that medical centers are experiencing offering the initiatives, such as the lack of adequate administrative support as reported to us by medical centers in our review. A system-wide evaluation could help ensure that VHA's recruitment and retention initiatives are effective in meeting departmental goals and that resources are effectively allocated across all VA medical centers. Evaluation results could also be useful if communicated to relevant stakeholders, such as medical centers, to inform them of any compliance issues or any operational changes that may be needed. Under federal internal control standards, relevant program information and guidance are needed throughout an agency to achieve all of its objectives, and should be communicated to management and others within the organization in a reliable form and within a time frame that enables them to carry out their organizational responsibilities, such as the implementation of a program or policy.

CONCLUSION

Adequate numbers of qualified nurses are essential for VHA to meet its mission of providing quality and timely health care for veterans. As the number of veterans seeking health care increases and the demographics of that population continue to change, VHA faces challenges ensuring it has the appropriate nurse workforce needed to provide care, including more complex, specialized services. In addition, the Choice Act required VHA to add additional clinical staff, including nurses, to its workforce to increase access to care for veterans. VHA has a number of key initiatives to help medical centers recruit and retain nurses; however, challenges, including competition with the private sector for qualified and skilled nurses and the lack of sufficient administrative support, may limit their effectiveness.

Furthermore, VHA's limited oversight of its key nurse recruitment and retention initiatives hinders its ability to assess the effectiveness of these initiatives and make any needed adjustments to help ensure its nurse workforce is keeping pace with the health care needs of veterans. Because of its limited monitoring, VHA lacks assurance that its medical centers are offering recruitment and retention initiatives in accordance with the policies and guidance that it has developed. Further, limited evaluations of medical centers offering VHA's initiatives have meant VHA is unable to systematically identify problems or needed program changes to ensure that the initiatives are being offered efficiently and effectively, including determining whether medical centers have sufficient training resources to support its nurse recruitment and retention initiatives. Further, without system-wide evaluations of its collective initiatives, VHA is unable to determine to what extent its nurse recruitment and retention initiatives are effective in meeting VHA polices and Choice Act provisions, or ultimately, whether VHA's initiatives are sufficient to meet veterans' health care needs.

RECOMMENDATIONS FOR EXECUTIVE ACTION

To help ensure the effective recruitment and retention of nurses across VA medical centers, we recommend the Secretary of Veterans Affairs direct the Under Secretary for Health to take the following three actions:

1) Develop a periodic reporting process to help monitor VA medical center compliance with the policies and procedures for each of its key recruitment and retention initiatives;
2) Evaluate the adequacy of training resources provided to all nurse recruiters at VA medical centers to ensure that they have the tools and information to perform their duties efficiently and effectively; and
3) Conduct a system-wide evaluation of VHA's key nurse recruitment and retention initiatives, to determine the overall effectiveness of these initiatives, including any needed improvements, and communicate results and information in a timely manner to relevant stakeholders.

AGENCY COMMENTS

We provided a draft of this report to VA for comment. In its written comments, VA generally agreed with our conclusions and concurred with our recommendations. In its comments, VA also provided information on workgroups it was planning to establish, as well as its plans for implementing each recommendation, with an estimated completion date of October 2017.

Sincerely yours,

Debra A. Draper
Director, Health Care

APPENDIX I: SELECTED CHARACTERISTICS OF VETERANS HEALTH ADMINISTRATION'S (VHA) NURSE WORKFORCE

Table 4. Number of Veterans Health Administration (VHA) Nurses Providing Direct and Indirect Care, by Position Type, Fiscal Year (FY) 2010 through FY 2014

Position type		FY 2010	FY 2011	FY 2012	FY 2013	FY 2014
Nurse practitioner	Direct	4,198	4,316	4,480	4,630	4,822
	Indirect	48	53	55	67	59
Registered nurse	Direct	45,289	46,464	47,651	49,798	52,178
	Indirect	2,493	2,508	2,516	2,628	2,789
Licensed practical nurse	Direct	12,909	13,238	13,479	13,834	14,169
	Indirect	42	52	48	69	75
Nursing assistant	Direct	9,852	10,049	10,370	10,811	10,987
	Indirect	20	14	12	26	17
Total	Direct	72,248	74,067	75,980	79,073	82,156
	Indirect	2,603	2,627	2,631	2,790	2,940

Source: VHA. | GAO-15-794

Note: Nurses within VHA provide both direct and indirect care to patients. Direct care includes any services that are provided to a veteran at the bedside; indirect care includes administrative and clerical duties that support direct patient care. All direct care services are provided at VA medical centers. Indirect care services can be provided at VA medical centers, Veterans Integrated Service Networks, or VA's central office.

Table 5. Number of Nurse Workforce Hires and Losses for FY 2015 at VA Medical Centers, by Position Type, as of June 2015

Position type	Number of nurse hires	Number of nurse losses
Nurse practitioner	431	291
Registered nurse	5,104	3,103
Licensed practical nurse	1,371	816
Nursing assistant	1,671	746
Total	8,577	4,956

Source: Veterans Health Administration (VHA). | GAO-15-794

Note: VHA nurse hires refers to the number of nurses that have come on board and are providing services at VA medical centers. Nurse workforce losses refers to the number of nurses who have left the VHA system for any reason, including retirements, death, termination or voluntary separation that removes a nurse employee from VHA; the loss numbers exclude VHA internal transfers.

Table 6. Veterans Health Administration (VHA) Nurse Turnover Rates by Position Type, Fiscal Year (FY) 2010 through FY 2014

Position type	FY 2010	FY 2011	FY 2012	FY 2013	FY 2014	5-year average
Nurse practitioner (NP)	5.8%	6.4%	7.2%	9.1%	9.1%	7.5%
Registered nurse (RN)[a]	6.4	6.9	7.5	7.8	7.8	7.3
Licensed practical nurse	6.9	7.8	8.3	8.4	7.9	7.9
Nursing assistant	10.1	9.2	8.7	8.8	8.9	9.2
Total	7.0	7.4	7.8	8.0	7.9	7.6

Source: VHA. | GAO-15-794

Note: The nurse turnover rate includes any loss, such as retirement, death, termination, or voluntary separation that removes a nurse employee from VHA; the loss numbers exclude VHA internal transfers.

[a] When reporting turnover rates for RNs, VHA includes NPs because NPs are RNs with additional credentials and education.

APPENDIX II: SELECTED CHARACTERISTICS OF VETERANS HEALTH ADMINISTRATION'S (VHA) KEY NURSE RECRUITMENT AND RETENTION INITIATIVES

			Expenditures (Number of participating nurses)		
Initiative	FY 2010	FY 2011	FY 2012	FY 2013	FY 2014
Education and training initiatives					
RN Transition to Practice[a]	n/a(n/a)	n/a(n/a)	n/a(n/a)	n/a(n/a)	n/a(n/a)
VA Learning Opportunities Residency	2,856,845 (335)	3,194,961 (349)	3,128,159 (368)	3,675,841 (434)	3,999,113 (475)
VA Nursing Academic Partnerships[b]	16,162,888 (640)	14,829,597 (440)	8,479,674 (260)	10,590,642 (162)	10,950,556 (366)
VA Nursing Academic Partnerships – Graduate Education[c]	n/a(n/a)	n/a(n/a)	n/a(n/a)	n/a(n/a)	427,469(5)

(Continued)

Initiative	Expenditures (Number of participating nurses)				
	FY 2010	FY 2011	FY 2012	FY 2013	FY 2014
Financial benefits and incentives initiatives					
Recruitment, retention, and relocation incentives	35,976,421 (6,514)	31,355,259 (5,358)	24,214,577 (5,880)	16,345,604 (2,692)	11,243,725 (1,899)
Education Debt Reduction Program[d]	5,938,084 (1,607)	5,554,648 (1,353)	6,015,672 (1,300)	4,599,492 (961)	3,079,405 (643)
Employee Incentive Scholarship Program[e]	30,965,399 (3,483)	30,006,001 (3,697)	23,353,940 (3,699)	20,701,054 (3,445)	23,806,109 (2,965)
Flexible work schedules[f]	n/a(n/a)	n/a(n/a)	n/a(n/a)	n/a(n/a)	n/a(n/a)

Source: VHA. | GAO-15-794

Note: The term expenditure refers to the actual spending of money, also known as an outlay. Participation refers to the number of VHA nurses who participate in the initiative; VHA nurses may be represented more than once in the table because nurses are allowed to participate in multiple initiatives.

[a]Expenditure data are not available because VHA does not provide specific funding to medical centers to offer this initiative; funding allocations are the responsibility of individual medical centers. Participation data are not available because VHA does not collect data on the number of nurses who participate in this initiative.

[b]In 2011, VHA introduced the Post-Baccalaureate Nurse Residency as a stand-alone initiative for academic year 2012-2013. In 2015, VHA rolled the residency into the existing VA Nursing Academic Partnerships initiative for new applicants to begin in academic year 2015-2016. The number of participating nurses in FY 2013 and FY 2014 reflects the number of participants in both the residency and the partnerships in academic years 2012-2013 and 2013-2014, respectively.

[c]In 2013, VHA introduced the Psychiatric Mental Health Nurse Practitioner Residency as a standalone initiative for academic year 2013-2014. In 2015, VHA introduced a graduate-education initiative—the VA Nursing Academic Partnerships – Graduate Education—into which it rolled the residency for new applicants. The number of participating nurses in FY 2014 reflects the number of participants in the residency in academic year 2013-2014.

[d]VHA nurses may be represented in more than one fiscal year because nurses can participate in the program for up to 5 contract years.

[e]VHA nurses may be represented in more than one fiscal year because nurses can participate in the program for up to 3 contract years.

[f]Expenditure data are not available because funding for flexible work schedules is accounted for in medical centers' budgets for salaries and wages. Participation data are not available because VHA does not collect data on the number of nurses who participate in this initiative.

End Notes

[1] See GAO, VA Health Care: Actions Needed to Ensure Adequate and Qualified Nurse Staffing, GAO-15-61 (Washington, D.C.: Oct. 16, 2014).

[2] U.S. Department of Health and Human Services, Health Resources and Services Administration, National Center for Health Workforce Analysis. The Future of the Nursing Workforce: National- and State-Level Projections, 2012-2015. Rockville, Md.: 2014.

[3] Pub. L. No.113-146, §§ 801(a)-(b) and 802(c), 128 Stat.1754,1801-1802 (Aug. 7, 2014).

[4] The VHA occupation with the highest staffing shortage was physicians. See Department of Veterans Affairs, Office of Inspector General, OIG Determination of Veterans Health Administration's Occupational Staffing Shortages, Report No. 15-00430-103 (Washington, D.C.: Jan. 30, 2015).

[5] Funding levels for the initiatives are the amounts expended on the initiatives.

[6] Each of VHA's 21 VISNs is responsible for managing and overseeing VA medical centers within a defined geographic area.

[7] The nurse turnover rate includes any loss, such as retirement, death, termination or voluntary separation that removes a nurse employee from VHA. The average nurse turnover rates were calculated for FY 2009 through FY 2013 for all nurses within VHA, regardless of position. The national average turnover rate over this 5-year period was 7.2 percent. (Turnover data from FY 2009 through FY 2013 were the most recent data available at the time we selected our sites.) VA assigns each medical center a complexity score derived from multiple variables to measure facility complexity arrayed along four categories, namely patient population served, clinical services offered, education and research complexity, and administrative complexity.

[8] We interviewed representatives from the following veterans service organizations: Disabled American Veterans and Paralyzed Veterans of America; from the following nursing organizations: American Psychiatric Nurses Association, Nurses Organization of VA, and Veteran's Administration Nurse Recruiters Association; and from the following unions that represent nurses at the medical centers included in our review: American Federation of Government Employees and Laborers' International Union of North America.

[9] See GAO, Standards for Internal Control in the Federal Government, GAO/AIMD-00-21.3.1 (Washington, D.C.: November 1999); Internal Control Management and Evaluation Tool, GAO-01-1008G (Washington, D.C.: August 2001). Internal control is synonymous with management control and comprises the plans, methods, and procedures used to meet missions, goals, and objectives.

[10] GAO, Managing For Results: GPRA Modernization Act Implementation Provides Important Opportunities to Address Government Challenges, GAO-11-617T (Washington, D.C.: May 10, 2011); Executive Guide: Effectively Implementing the Government Performance and Results Act, GAO/GGD-96-118 (Washington, D.C.: June 1996); Managing For Results: Executive Branch Should More Fully Implement the GPRA Modernization Act to Address Pressing Governance Challenges, GAO-13-518 (Washington, D.C.: June 26, 2013).

[11] Department of Veterans Affairs, Veterans Health Administration, 2014 Interim Workforce and Succession Strategic Plan (Washington, D.C.: 2014).

[12] Direct care includes any services that are provided to a veteran at the bedside; indirect care includes administrative and clerical duties that support direct patient care. All direct care services are provided at VA medical centers. Indirect care services can be provided at VA medical centers, VISNs, or VA's central office.

[13] Under statutory authority, VA establishes the education requirements of its health care practitioners, including NPs, RNs, LPNs, and NAs. See 38 U.S.C. § 7401.

[14] The overall nurse workforce turnover rate at each of the VA medical centers ranged from 2 percent to 17 percent in FY 2014.

[15] USAjobs.gov is the federal government's official website that advertises vacant positions. The website also provides information about federal occupations and allows candidates to apply for vacant positions online.

[16] Onboarding and credentialing is the process that health professional candidates must complete before they can begin working at VA medical centers. This process involves several steps, including VHA verifying candidates' work experience and credentials, and candidates completing a physical examination.

[17] VHA has other initiatives that may aid in the recruitment and retention of nurses, such as special advancements for performance or nursing achievements. For the purposes of this report, we focused on VHA's initiatives whose primary goals included nurse recruitment and retention.

[18] In 2011, VHA introduced the Post-Baccalaureate Nurse Residency as a stand-alone initiative. In 2015, VHA rolled this initiative into the VA Nursing Academic Partnerships for new applicants to begin in academic year 2015-2016.

[19] According to officials, the medical center offered flexible work schedules in some, but not all, of its units.

[20] We previously reported on the availability of flexible work schedules at VA. See GAO, VA Health Care: Improved Staffing Methods and Greater Availability of Alternate and Flexible Work Schedules Could Enhance the Recruitment and Retention of Inpatient Nurses, GAO-09-17 (Washington, D.C.: Oct. 24, 2008).

[21] In November 2011, VHA issued a directive establishing as VHA policy that VA medical centers offer the RN Transition to Practice initiative. Department of Veterans Affairs, VHA Registered Nurses (RN) Transition-to-Practice Program, VHA Directive 2011-039 (Washington, D.C.: Nov. 23, 2011).

[22] Pub. L. No 113-146, § 302(b), 128 Stat. 1754, 1788 (Aug. 7, 2014), codified at 38 U.S.C. § 7683(d).

[23] GAO/AIMD-00-21.3.1.

[24] GAO/AIMD-00.21.3.1.

[25] Department of Veterans Affairs, Veterans Health Administration, 2014 Interim Workforce and Succession Strategic Plan (Washington, D.C.: 2014).

[26] VHA's Healthcare Talent Management manages the VA Learning Opportunities Residency, the Education Debt Reduction Program, and the Employee Incentive Scholarship Program, which includes the National Nursing Education Initiative and the VA National Education for Employees Program.

[27] Department of Veterans Affairs, Veterans Health Administration, 2014 Interim Workforce and Succession Strategic Plan (Washington, D.C.: 2014).

[28] Department of Veterans Affairs, Department of Veterans Affairs Annual Report On the Use of Authorities to Enhance Retention of Experienced Nurses for Fiscal Year 2014 (Washington, D.C.: 2015).

In: Nurse Staffing Within the Veterans Health ... ISBN: 978-1-63485-264-7
Editor: Eugene Glover © 2016 Nova Science Publishers, Inc.

Chapter 2

VA HEALTH CARE: ACTIONS NEEDED TO ENSURE ADEQUATE AND QUALIFIED NURSE STAFFING[*]

United States Government Accountability Office

WHY GAO DID THIS STUDY

GAO and others have raised prior concerns about the adequacy and qualifications of VHA's nurse staffing. In part to address these concerns, VHA issued a directive in 2010 requiring all VAMCs to implement a standardized methodology for determining an adequate and qualified nurse workforce, which includes developing and executing nurse staffing plans. It also requires VAMCs to use the methodology on an ongoing basis to evaluate staffing plans.

GAO was asked to provide information on nurse staffing at VAMCs. This report reviews the extent to which (1) VAMCs have implemented VHA's nurse staffing methodology, and (2) VHA oversees VAMCs' implementation and ongoing administration of the methodology. GAO reviewed documents and interviewed officials from VHA, seven VAMCs selected to ensure variation in factors such as geographic location, and regional offices for these VAMCs. GAO used federal internal control standards to evaluate VHA's

---

[*] This is an edited, reformatted and augmented version of a United States Government Accountability Office, Publication No. GAO-15-61, dated October 2014.

oversight. GAO also interviewed representatives of veterans service organizations, nursing organizations, and unions.

WHAT GAO RECOMMENDS

GAO recommends VA: (1) assess VAMCs' ability to implement the methodology, (2) monitor VAMCs' ongoing compliance with the methodology, (3) complete timely evaluations, (4) improve the timeliness of communication with VAMCs, and (5) define areas of responsibility and reporting within VA's management structure. VA concurred with the recommendations.

WHAT GAO FOUND

The seven Department of Veterans Affairs medical centers (VAMC) in GAO's review implemented the Veterans Health Administration's (VHA) nurse staffing methodology, experienced problems developing and executing the related nurse staffing plans, and some reported improvements in nurse staffing. Specifically, GAO found that each of the seven VAMCs had developed a facility-wide staffing plan—which outlines initiatives needed to ensure appropriate unit-level nurse staffing and skill mix—and taken steps to execute it. However, VAMCs experienced problems—such as lack of data resources and difficulties with training—in both the development and execution of their staffing plans. Some VAMC staff reported improvements in the adequacy and qualifications of their units' nursing staff when nurse staffing plan initiatives were executed. For example, at two VAMCs where the number of nurses was increased or where support services for nurses were put in place, such as a designated group of staff to assist in transporting patients to and from appointments off the unit, unit staff said the adequacy of the nursing staff had improved. However, some VAMC unit staff reported that unit nurse staffing continued to be inadequate and that nurse unit assignments and job duties were not always appropriate for their qualifications.

VHA's oversight is limited for ensuring its nurse staffing methodology is implemented and administered appropriately. GAO found the following internal controls were limited in VHA's oversight process:

- **Environmental assessment.** VHA did not comprehensively assess each VAMC to ensure preparedness for implementing the methodology, including having the necessary technical support and resources, prior to the issuance of the directive requiring each VAMC to implement the methodology.
- **Monitoring compliance.** VHA does not have a plan for monitoring VAMCs to ensure compliance with the implementation and ongoing administration of the methodology.
- **Evaluation.** VHA has conducted limited evaluations of the methodology, and at least one of these evaluations has been significantly delayed.
- **Timeliness of communication.** VHA's protracted timeline for communicating methodology-related information may have hindered the ability of VAMCs to appropriately develop their staffing plans and to execute the initiatives contained in those plans.
- **Organizational accountability.** VHA did not define areas of responsibility or establish the appropriate line of reporting within VA's management structure for oversight of the implementation and ongoing administration of the methodology.

Without these internal controls in place, VHA cannot ensure its methodology meets department goals, such as establishing a standardized methodology for determining an adequate and qualified nurse workforce at VAMCs, and ultimately, having nurse staffing that is adequate to meet veterans' growing and increasingly complex health care needs.

ABBREVIATIONS

FY	fiscal year
LPN	licensed practical nurse
NA	nursing assistant
NDNQI	National Database of Nursing Quality Indicators
NHPPD	nursing hours per patient day
OIG	Office of Inspector General
ONS	Office of Nursing Services
RN	registered nurse

VA	Department of Veterans Affairs
VAMC	VA medical center
VHA	Veterans Health Administration
VISN	Veterans Integrated Service Network

* * *

October 16, 2014

The Honorable Mike Coffman
Chairman
Subcommittee on Oversight & Investigations
Committee on Veterans' Affairs
House of Representatives

Dear Mr. Chairman:

The Department of Veterans Affairs' (VA) Veterans Health Administration (VHA) provides medical care to millions of veterans each year. Nurses play an essential role in the medical care that veterans receive, and it is critical that VHA has an adequate and qualified nursing staff to meet veterans' needs. Studies have shown that better care is provided when facilities have both an adequate number of nurses, and nurses that are appropriately qualified for the jobs to which they are assigned.[1] According to VHA, it employs more than 80,000 nurses, making it the largest employer of nurses in the country. The number of veterans receiving care at VA medical centers (VAMC) increased from 5.2 million in fiscal year (FY) 2009 to 5.8 million in FY 2013, and VHA estimates that it will serve close to 8.8 million veterans by 2020. Furthermore, more intensive nursing care is being required by a growing number of veterans returning from military operations in Afghanistan and Iraq, and by aging veterans from prior eras of service.

For more than 10 years, concerns have been raised that VHA might not have an adequate and qualified nursing staff to care for the increasing number of veterans requiring more complex care. In 2002, Congress passed legislation requiring VA to develop a nationwide policy on staffing levels for the operation of VAMCs.[2] Specifically, the law required VA to establish a nationwide policy on the staffing of VAMCs to ensure they have adequate staff, taking into account staffing levels and the mixture of staff skills required for providing care to veterans. The need for a new nurse staffing policy was highlighted in 2004 when VA's Office of Inspector General (OIG) issued a report raising concerns about the adequacy of nurse staffing levels in VAMCs' inpatient units.[3] By 2008, however, no national policy on nurse staffing had been implemented. In October 2008, we issued a report raising concerns about the adequacy of nurse staffing, specifically for registered nurses (RN) in inpatient units, and the need to expeditiously proceed with developing and implementing a new nurse staffing system, among other issues.[4] We recommended that VHA develop a detailed plan for implementing a new nurse staffing system and ensure it provided accurate nurse staffing estimates. In part to address these concerns, in 2010, VHA issued a directive requiring each VAMC to implement a nationally standardized methodology for determining an adequate and qualified nurse workforce, which includes the development and execution of nurse staffing plans. The staffing plans outline initiatives needed to ensure appropriate nurse staffing levels and skill mix in units to support high-quality patient care in the most effective manner possible. The directive also requires VAMCs to use the methodology on an ongoing basis to evaluate staffing plans at least annually.

You expressed interest in obtaining information on nurse staffing at VAMCs. In this report, we review the extent to which (1) VAMCs have implemented VHA's nurse staffing methodology, and (2) VHA oversees VAMCs' implementation and ongoing administration of its nurse staffing methodology.

To determine the extent to which VAMCs have implemented VHA's nurse staffing methodology, we reviewed documents and interviewed officials from VHA. Specifically, we reviewed information and interviewed officials from VHA's Office of Nursing Services (ONS)—the VHA office responsible for providing national policies, guidelines, and oversight for all VAMC nursing personnel—on the extent to which VAMCs have implemented the methodology in inpatient units (Phase I); VAMCs have piloted the methodology in operating room, emergency department, and spinal cord injury units (Phase II); and VHA has developed plans for an automatic staffing system (Phase III). We interviewed officials and nursing staff from seven VAMCs located in: (1) Battle Creek, Michigan; (2) Bronx, New York; (3) Columbia, South Carolina; (4) Dallas, Texas, (5) Fort Harrison, Montana; (6) San Diego, California; and (7) Tampa, Florida about their experiences implementing VHA's nurse staffing methodology. These VAMCs were selected to ensure variation in factors such as geographic location, rural versus urban location, complexity,[5] RN turnover rate, and Magnet status.[6] We did not independently assess the extent to which the VAMCs' implementation of the staffing methodology contributed to an adequate and qualified workforce. Furthermore, the results of our review of the seven VAMCs are not generalizable across all VAMCs. We reviewed literature and interviewed researchers who have published in the area of nurse staffing, representatives of selected veterans service organizations,[7] and representatives of selected nursing organizations and unions[8] to gain their perspectives about the current environment for nurse staffing, nurse staffing methodologies in general, and VHA's nurse staffing methodology.

To determine the extent to which VHA oversees VAMCs' implementation and ongoing administration of its nurse staffing methodology, we reviewed documents and interviewed officials from VHA. Specifically, we reviewed VHA documents, such as national directives, policies, and evaluation plans, to determine the extent to which VHA has provided VAMCs guidance regarding the implementation and ongoing administration of the staffing methodology. We interviewed officials from ONS, the seven VAMCs in our review, and the regional Veterans Integrated Service Networks (VISN)[9] for these seven VAMCs regarding their oversight of VAMCs' implementation of the staffing methodology. We also interviewed ONS officials and VAMC officials and staff about the extent to which VAMCs' implementation of the staffing methodology contributes to an adequate and qualified nurse workforce. To determine whether VHA applied appropriate internal controls in its oversight of the nurse staffing methodology, we used relevant criteria from federal internal control standards. We also used relevant strategic planning and performance measures from the Government Performance and Results Act as enhanced by the Government Performance and Results Modernization Act of 2010, as incorporated in GAO's guidance on assessing performance.[10]

We conducted this performance audit from September 2013 to October 2014 in accordance with generally accepted government auditing standards. Those standards require that we plan and perform the audit to obtain sufficient, appropriate evidence to provide a reasonable basis for our findings and conclusions based on our audit objectives. We believe that the evidence obtained provides a reasonable basis for our findings and conclusions based on our audit objectives.

BACKGROUND

Nurse staffing is a critical part of health care because of the effects it can have on patient outcomes and nurse job satisfaction. According to VHA, its staffing methodology aims to maximize nurses' productivity and efficiency, while providing safe patient care by ensuring appropriate nurse staffing levels and skill mix.

VHA Nurse Workforce

VHA's nurse workforce is primarily composed of RNs,[11] licensed practical nurses (LPN),[12] and nursing assistants (NA). These nurses provide care—ranging from primary care to complex specialty care—in inpatient, outpatient, and residential care settings at 151 VAMCs across the country.[13] In addition to the size of the nursing workforce, the nursing skill mix—i.e., the share of each type of nurse (RNs, LPNs, or NAs) of the total—is an important component of nurse staffing. Units vary in their nursing skill mix, depending on the needs of their patients. For example, intensive care units require higher intensity nursing, and may have a skill mix that is primarily composed of RNs compared to other types of nursing units that may provide less complex care. (See table 1 for a general description of the types of nursing staff position, responsibilities, and educational requirements.)

Although the number of nurses at VAMCs increased from FY 2009 to FY 2013, VHA ranked nurses as the second most challenging occupation to recruit and retain. Specifically, the total number of nurses at VAMCs increased 13 percent from 72,542 in FY 2009 to 81,940 in FY 2013, with similarly proportionate increases within each position type—RN, LPN, and NA. During the same time period, the annual nurse turnover rate at VAMCs—the percentage of nurses who left VHA through retirement, death, termination, or voluntary separation—increased from 6.6 percent to 8.0 percent. Although RNs had the lowest turnover rate among nurses, VHA noted particular difficulty recruiting and retaining for the position, particularly for RNs with advanced professional skills, knowledge, and experience, such as RNs that provide services in medical and surgical care units.[14] VHA projects that approximately 40,000 new nurses will be needed through FY 2018 to maintain current staffing levels and to meet the needs of veterans.

Table 1. Types of Nursing Staff Position, Responsibilities, and Educational Requirements

Position type	Responsibilities	Educational requirements
Registered nurse (RN)	Assesses and provides care to patients, administers medications; documents patients' medical conditions, including admissions and discharges; analyzes test results; establishes treatment plans; and operates medical equipment.	Highest educational requirements: Has completed a nursing education program, met state licensing requirements, and passed a nurse licensing examination to obtain an RN license.
Licensed practical nurse (LPN)[a]	Takes patient vital signs, provides basic care, and administers medications, but generally does not provide certain complex patient care services such as patient assessments or administration of intravenous medications.	Fewer educational requirements than RNs: Has a high school diploma or its equivalent and passed a licensing examination upon completion of a state-approved program available at technical schools and community colleges, typically lasting 1 year.
Nursing assistant	Attends to basic patient needs such as providing personal care to patients (e.g., assistance with bathing, dressing, and personal hygiene), carries out non-specialized duties (e.g., measure blood pressure), and supports other nursing staff.	Less extensive educational requirements than RNs and LPNs: Has registered as a nursing assistant with their state health department, and passed a written competency examination upon completion of a state-approved training program, generally lasting 3 to 12 weeks.

Source: VHA, nursing organizations, and literature. I GAO-15-61

[a] LPNs and licensed vocational nurses have the same level of education and patient care responsibilities. In this table, when we refer to LPNs, we are referring to both LPNs and licensed vocational nurses.

VHA's Nurse Staffing Methodology

To help ensure adequate and qualified nurse staffing at VAMCs, in July 2010, VHA issued *VHA Directive 2010-034: Staffing Methodology for VHA Nursing Personnel*. ONS, the VHA office responsible for providing national policies and guidelines for all VHA nursing personnel, led the development of the nurse staffing methodology, which began in 2007. (See figure 1.)

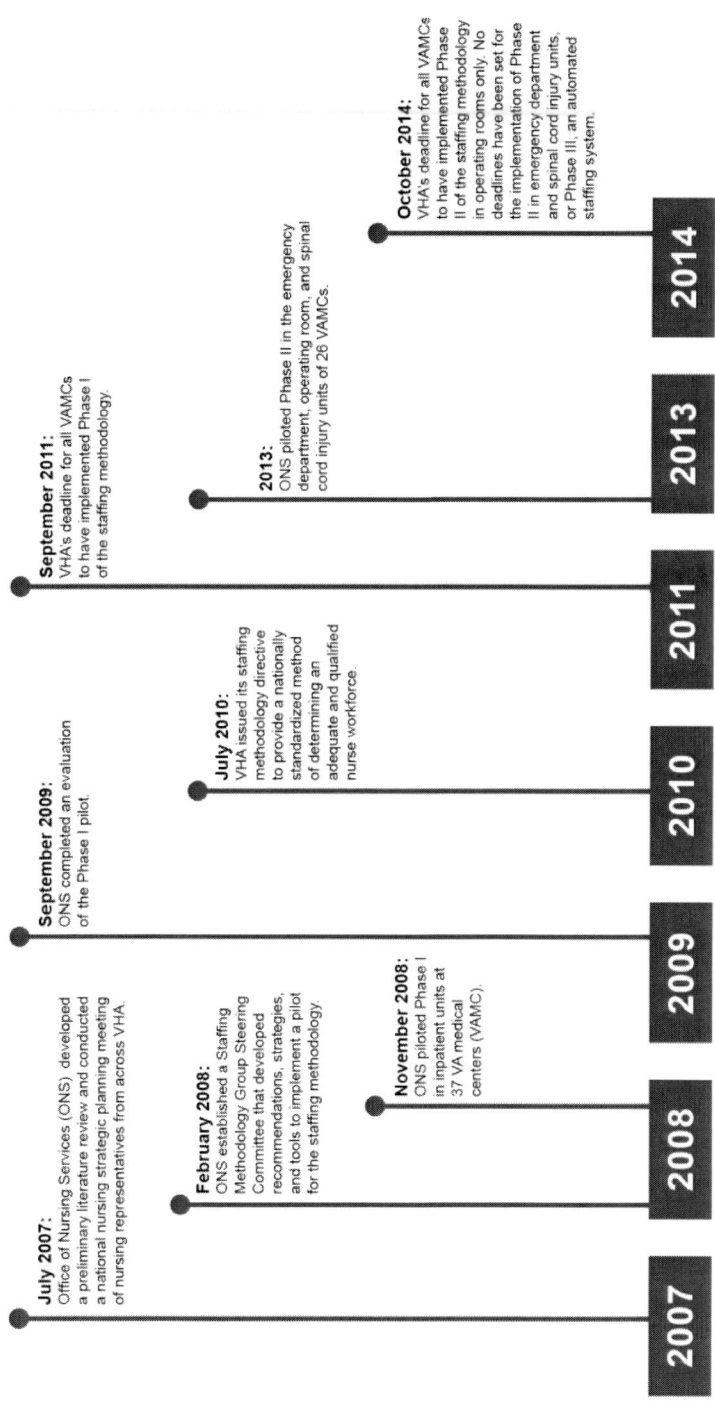

Figure 1. Timeline for Development and Implementation of the Veterans Health Administration's (VHA) Nurse Staffing Methodology.

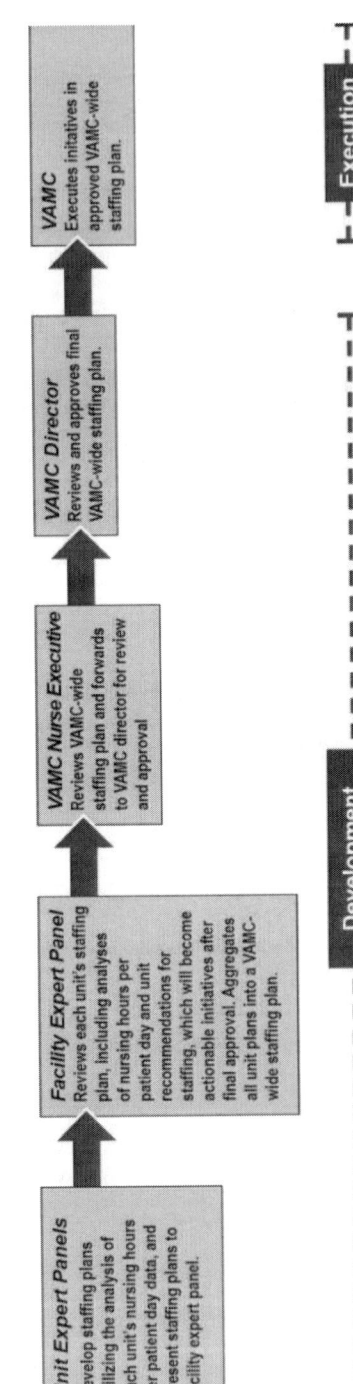

Source: VHA. | GAO-15-61

Figure 2. VA Medical Center (VAMC) Process for Implementing the Veterans Health Administration's (VHA) Nurse Staffing Methodology.

To implement the methodology, each VAMC is required to (1) develop a VAMC-wide staffing plan for its nurse workforce, comprised of individual unit-level staffing plans, and (2) execute that plan. (See figure 2 for an outline of the process for implementing VHA's nurse staffing methodology.)

Each VAMC unit is to develop a staffing plan outlining recommendations on the appropriate nurse staffing levels and skill mix needed in that unit to support high-quality patient care in the most effective manner possible. Specifically, staffing plans are to be developed using expert panels and a data-driven analysis of nursing hours per patient day (NHPPD). VAMC nurse executives—members of senior management within each VAMC— are responsible for implementing the staffing methodology in their respective VAMCs.

- Expert panels: advisory groups—at the unit and facility level—of VAMC staff with in-depth knowledge of nurse staffing needs. The use of expert panels is intended to apply principles of shared governance, which allows nurses to have influence over the delivery of patient care and involves stakeholders from across the VAMC. VAMC nurse executives are responsible for ensuring that the unit-based expert panels represent all nursing types (RN, LPN, NA) and developing the VAMC's facility expert panel.
- Data-driven analysis of NHPPD: involves determining the number and skill mix of nurses needed for each unit by calculating the number of direct patient care nursing hours provided for all patients on that unit during a 24-hour period.[15] The use of NHPPD represents a move away from the more traditional nurse-to-patient ratios that assign a certain number of patients to each nurse. Some research suggests that NHPPD can better capture changes in nurses' workloads and case mix resulting from admissions and discharges, as well as patient acuity levels, which can impact the amount of time nurses spend with each patient.[16]

After developing the staffing plan, each unit-based expert panel presents its plan, which includes staffing recommendations, to the VAMC's facility expert panel. Those staffing recommendations may include, for example, initiatives to change the number and skill mix of nurses needed for each shift; change the number of nurses required for coverage during predicted absences, such as annual and sick leave; and develop support services for nurses, such as designated individuals to transport patients to other areas of the facility as needed. The facility expert panel—comprised of staff from across the VAMC—reviews each unit-based panel's staffing plan and aggregates all of the unit plans into one VAMC-wide staffing plan. The VAMC nurse executive reviews the VAMC-wide staffing plan and forwards it to the VAMC director for review and approval. Once approved, the VAMC then begins execution of the initiatives outlined in the VAMC-wide staffing plan. The directive requires each VAMC to conduct an ongoing staffing analysis to evaluate staffing plans annually, at a minimum, and for VAMC directors to incorporate projected staffing needs into their annual budget review.

The staffing methodology is being implemented in three phases.

- In Phase I, VAMCs were to implement the staffing methodology in all inpatient units no later than September 30, 2011.
- In Phase II, VAMCs are to implement the staffing methodology for all other units, including the operating room, emergency department, and spinal cord injury units.[17] ONS has completed the Phase II pilot for operating room units, and VAMCs are expected to implement the methodology in their operating room units by October 1, 2014. Deadlines for the implementation in other Phase II units have not been set.
- In Phase III, VAMCs are to use an automated system developed by VHA that (1) merges VHA staffing data used in the staffing methodology and other VHA data, such as human resource data, into one data system, and (2) incorporates the data into staffing-related reports, such as quality-of-care reports. A deadline for Phase III implementation has not been set.

In May 2014, the VA OIG found that VAMCs in its review varied in their implementation of the staffing methodology. Specifically, the VA OIG reported that 8 of the 28 VAMCs reviewed had not fully implemented all components of the staffing methodology by September 2013, 2 years past the implementation date required by the VHA directive.[18] As these findings were similar to those of its April 2013 report,[19] the VA OIG stated in its 2014 report, "We re-emphasize the need for all facilities to fully implement the methodology and accurately address patient needs with safe and adequate staffing."

Impact of Nurse Staffing on Patient Outcomes and Nurse Job Satisfaction

Adequate and qualified nurse staffing at VAMCs is required to provide effective and continuous patient care and to maintain a stable and engaged workplace. The importance of nurse staffing on patient outcomes and nurse job satisfaction has been emphasized by various entities, including The Joint Commission;[20] American Nurses Association;[21] Institute of Medicine;[22] and Agency for Healthcare Research and Quality.[23] Additionally, research has linked the adequacy and qualifications of nurse staffing to patient outcomes and nurse job satisfaction. For example, studies have shown:

- A link between the adequacy of nurse staffing and patient outcomes, particularly in inpatient units, such as intensive care and surgical units. For example, medication errors, pressure ulcers, hospital acquired infections, pneumonia, longer-than-expected stays, and higher mortality rates each have been associated with inadequate nurse staffing.[24]
- A link between the qualifications of nursing staff and patient outcomes. For example, one study found that patients cared for in units utilizing more licensed and experienced nursing staff (RNs and LPNs) and fewer unlicensed aides (NAs) had shorter lengths of stay.[25] Other studies linked baccalaureate-prepared nurses to lower mortality rates.[26]
- A link between nurse staffing and job satisfaction. For example, some studies have linked low job satisfaction to heavy workloads and an inability to ensure patient safety.[27] Other studies found that improving nurse staffing and working conditions may simultaneously reduce nurses' burnout, risk of turnover, and the likelihood of medical errors, while increasing patients' satisfaction with their care.[28]

Non-VA health care organizations use various approaches to ensure effective nurse staffing. For example, some use fixed nurse-to-patient ratios while others use adjustable, unit-specific minimum staffing levels,[29] and there have been several efforts to address nurse staffing using these different approaches.[30] For example, California has enacted legislation requiring regulations that mandate specific nurse-to-patient ratios that limit the number of patients cared for by an individual nurse. Other states have passed legislation or adopted regulations addressing nurse staffing without mandating specific ratios or staffing levels. For example, some states require hospitals to have committees responsible for developing unit staffing plans or require public reporting of staffing.

VAMCs IN OUR REVIEW IMPLEMENTED VHA'S NURSE STAFFING METHODOLOGY, EXPERIENCED PROBLEMS DEVELOPING AND EXECUTING STAFFING PLANS, AND SOME REPORTED IMPROVEMENTS IN NURSE STAFFING

All seven VAMCs in our review developed staffing plans using VHA's nurse staffing methodology and have taken steps to execute them. However, VAMCs experienced problems in both the development and execution of their staffing plans. Improvements in nurse staffing were reported by some of the VAMCs which had taken steps to execute the staffing plans.

VAMCs in Our Review Have Implemented VHA's Nurse Staffing Methodology by Developing Staffing Plans and Taking Steps to Execute Them

The seven VAMCs in our review have implemented VHA's nurse staffing methodology; specifically, each of these VAMCs has developed a facility-wide staffing plan, comprised of unit-level staffing plans for inpatient units, and has taken steps to execute it.[31] Although each of the seven VAMCs in our review developed a staffing plan for FY 2013, only one had developed a plan per VHA's directive—that is, used both expert panels and analysis of NHPPD—by September 30, 2011, the deadline specified in the directive. (See table 2.) Across all 151 VAMCs, according to ONS officials, VAMCs' implementation of the nurse staffing methodology varied, with, for example, some VAMCs completing the development of their staffing plans during FY 2013, and some only beginning the development process.

In addition to developing staffing plans, all seven VAMCs in our review had taken steps to execute their respective staffing plans. For example, VAMCs had taken steps to execute initiatives to increase the number of unit nurses or change the skill mix of nurses to address patient care needs. (See table 3 for examples of VAMCs' staffing plan initiatives.) VAMC officials told us there are many factors that could affect the execution of staffing plan initiatives, such as available resources, the amount of time needed, and other strategic priorities.

Table 2. VA Medical Center (VAMC) Status for Development of VAMC-Wide Staffing Plan

VAMC	Status FY 2011	FY 2012	FY 2013
A	●	●	●
B	o	●	●
C	o	●	●
D	o	o	●
E	o	o	●
F	o	●	●
G	o	●	●

Source: Seven VAMCs in our review. I GAO-15-61
● VAMC-wide staffing plan complete per Veterans Health Administration (VHA) directive.
o VAMC-wide staffing plan not complete per VHA directive.
Note: VHA Directive 2010-034 required each VAMC to develop a VAMC-wide staffing plan for use in its inpatient units by September 30, 2011. The process for developing the staffing plans included the use of expert panels—at the unit level and at the facility level—and a data-driven analysis of nursing hours per patient day.

Table 3. Examples of VA Medical Centers' (VAMC) Staffing Plan Initiatives

Initiative	Description
Number of nurses	Increase the total number of unit nurses—for example, registered nurses (RN), licensed practical nurses (LPN), or nursing assistants (NA)—to meet direct patient care needs.
Skill mix	Change skill mix of nurses to better meet patient needs—particularly having more RNs (rather than LPNs) to conduct timely patient assessments.
Contract nurse pool	Develop contracts to use temporary nursing staff from external employment organizations to meet short-term staffing needs.
Float pool	Develop designated group of nurses to float to units on an as-needed basis.
Sitter pool	Develop designated group of staff to provide one-on-one direct patient observation to allow nurses to bettercare for a broader group of patients.
Transport team	Develop designated group of staff to assist in transporting patients to and from appointments off the unit so that RNs are able to remain on the unit.
Staff reassignment	Reassign nursing staff from an overstaffed unit to an understaffed unit.
Patient census	Temporarily reduce patient census by closing beds because of inadequate staffing.

Source: Seven VAMCs in our review. I GAO-15-61

Table 4. Examples of Problems VA Medical Centers (VAMC) Experienced Developing and Executing Staffing Plans

	Problems developing staffing plans					Problems executing staffing plans	
VAMC	Lack of necessary data resources	Difficulty completing and understanding training	Time required	Lack of communication within VAMC	Difficulty integrating unit staff in expert panels	Hiring delays	Budget constraints
A		x	x			x	x
B	x	x	x	x	x	x	x
C	x		x	x	x	x	x
D	x	x	x	x		x	x
E	x	x	x			x	x
F	x	x	x	x	x	x	
G	x	x	x				

Source: Seven VAMCs in our review. I GAO-15-61

VAMCs Experienced Problems Developing and Executing Staffing Plans, and Many of These Problems Persist

Officials and nursing staff from the seven VAMCs in our review told us they experienced problems developing and executing staffing plans. (See table 4 for examples of problems.) Some VAMCs were able to devise solutions; however in many cases, the problems have persisted.

Problems Developing Staffing Plans

Staff and officials from each of the seven VAMCs in our review reported facing problems developing staffing plans.

- *Lack of necessary data resources.* Staff and officials at six of the seven VAMCs in our review said they did not have the appropriate data resources to effectively calculate NHPPD as required by VHA's staffing methodology directive. Specifically, the directive instructs VAMC staff to calculate NHPPD using a wide range of data, such as number of admissions, transfers, and discharges; hours used for planning and treatment; and human resources data. We found that staff and officials needed to use multiple sources to collect the necessary data, in some cases manually, a process they said was time-consuming and potentially error-prone, and required data expertise they did not always have. For example, at one VAMC, the staffing methodology coordinator—a VAMC official who assists with the administrative tasks associated with the implementation process—told us she struggled with some data analysis techniques, such as creating a spreadsheet to help track staffing data, but the VAMC did not have the financial resources to hire additional data analysts to support the methodology. In contrast, officials from two VAMCs in our review told us staffing methodology coordinators were assigned in part based on their data analysis expertise.
- *Difficulty completing and understanding training.* Staff from six of the seven VAMCs in our review said the ONS training on the methodology was time consuming to complete, and difficult to understand. In 2011, ONS switched from instructor-led, group training to individual, computer-based PowerPoint training. Many unit staff reported that because the computer-based training took many hours to complete, it was difficult to find the time to complete it, while also carrying out their patient care responsibilities. They told us

they often had to start and stop the training to attend to patients, which diminished its effectiveness. Further, the course's complex material was hard to absorb through an individual, computer-based course, with many staff suggesting their understanding would have been greatly improved with an instructor-led, group course where they could ask questions, ensure consistency of learning, and build camaraderie among unit expert panel members. To address the difficulties in completing and understanding the training, one VAMC developed its own instructor-led, group training provided to all its units.

- *Time required.* Staff and officials at all seven of the VAMCs in our review reported that developing staffing plans required a lot of staff time due to the complexity of the process. In particular, they said gaining an understanding of the methodology, collecting the necessary data, convening the unit expert panels, and preparing presentations for the facility expert panel were time-intensive tasks that, in some circumstances, took time away from patient care. For example, members from one unit expert panel estimated they spent, in total, about 160 hours (4 weeks) developing the unit staffing plan during the first year the staffing methodology was implemented in their unit. Some VAMCs' staffing methodology coordinators developed specific processes designed to decrease the burden on nursing staff and improve efficiency. For example, they created templates for unit panel members to use in staffing plan development; such templates improved efficiency because unit panel members did not have to independently develop their presentation format. Further, facility expert panel members had to orient themselves to only one template, and were therefore able to more easily make facility-level comparisons and decisions.

- *Lack of communication within VAMC.* Unit expert panel members at four of the seven VAMCs in our review said there was a lack of communication between nurses and VAMC leadership regarding the status of the staffing plans, including plans for execution of the staffing plan initiatives. Staff at one of these VAMCs said they had not received any feedback on their FY 2012 or FY 2013 unit staffing plans; they added that developing the 2013 staffing plan without getting any feedback on the prior year's plan felt "frustrating." In contrast, at another VAMC, officials told us that all unit staff—not

just staff involved in the unit panel—received regular updates on the nurse staffing process at their monthly unit staff meetings.
- *Difficulty integrating unit staff into expert panels.* Staff and officials at three VAMCs described challenges in integrating unit staff into expert panels. Some unit panel members told us that although they were considered members of their respective unit panels, they were not significantly involved in the development of their units' staffing plans. For example, a unit panel member said the VAMC's staffing methodology coordinator calculated the unit's NHPPD, developed the corresponding unit staffing plan, and presented the unit staffing plan to the respective facility expert panel almost entirely without her unit's input. As a result, there was limited involvement of the unit panel members in the expert panel and, consequently, limited shared governance. Officials at these VAMCs said that from their perspectives, there was interest in the methodology among unit panel members, but sometimes it was difficult for these staff to attend relevant meetings because of patient needs. In contrast, unit panel members at other VAMCs in our review described how they were fully integrated into the unit panels. They described in detail the data analyses they prepared, the meetings they participated in, and their experiences presenting their unit staffing plans to the facility expert panel. Members from one unit panel told us it was helpful to be able to use data to validate the unit's staffing and share this data with the facility expert panel—VAMC staff "beyond the typical chain of command." Officials at this VAMC noted that unit panel members felt "empowered" to present their work to the facility expert panels.

Problems Executing Staffing Plans

Staff and officials from six of the seven VAMCs in our review noted problems executing staffing plans once approved by the VAMC director.

- *Hiring delays.* Staff and officials from six of the seven VAMCs in our review said they often faced hiring delays that impacted their ability to execute staffing plan initiatives. Some VAMC staff noted it could take more than 6 months to fill unit vacancies. Although staff from one VAMC said hiring was slowed by the dearth of qualified nurses in their community, staff from other VAMCs in our review said the supply of nurses was not the problem, but rather the problem was the VHA hiring process, which took months to complete for each candidate. Additionally, VAMC staff noted that new hires also needed to complete necessary internal trainings before joining a unit full time, which added to the delays, and that some new hires were hurried through this training process because their units were so desperate to have them on staff.

- *Budget constraints.* Staff and officials from five of the seven VAMCs in our review said their VAMCs were not able to fully execute their staffing plans due to budget constraints. For example, at one VAMC, one of the approved staffing plan initiatives was the hiring of a large number of nurses for its units, in part, to address the VAMC's inability to increase their nursing staff over a period of years. The official told us that, due to budget constraints, the VAMC was going to phase in this hiring initiative over the next few years.

Improvements in Nurse Staffing Were Reported When VAMCs Executed Staffing Plan Initiatives

Some VAMC staff reported improvements in the adequacy and qualifications of their units' nursing staff when nurse staffing plan initiatives were executed. For example, at two VAMCs at which the number of nurses was increased or support services for nurses, such as patient transporters or sitters, were put in place,[32] unit staff said the adequacy of the nursing staff had improved. Furthermore, improvements in the qualifications of unit nursing staff were noted by staff in VAMC units where, for example, skill-mix changes were made or the amount of floating of nurses from their home unit to an unfamiliar unit was decreased. Both VAMC officials and unit staff noted improvements in staffing when nurses' qualifications were more appropriately matched to the right level of work (for example, having RNs rather than LPNs available to provide more complex patient care) and to the right units (for example, the units for which they were hired and trained).

Some VAMC staff said they also had seen improvements in patient outcomes and nurse job satisfaction. For example, nursing staff at one VAMC said that after creating sitter positions—as indicated by their VAMC's staffing plan—they saw a decrease in patient falls. The staff said sitters were able to monitor patients more closely, and as a result, patients were less likely to fall during walks to the bathroom, for example. Similarly, nursing staff in a mental health unit at another VAMC said that by having more staff they had decreased their restraint use because there were more staff available to meet veterans' needs. Additionally, nursing staff we interviewed at one VAMC that had made staffing changes based on staffing plans said they were better able to provide the type of nursing care "veterans deserve," and this made them feel more positive about their work. Some nurses at this VAMC also said the shared governance aspect of the methodology was empowering, which, combined with their enhanced understanding of staffing at their VAMC, helped improve their overall job satisfaction.

However, some VAMC unit staff reported that unit nurse staffing continued to be inadequate and that nurse unit assignments and job duties were not always appropriate for their qualifications. For six of the VAMCs in our review, staff from at least one unit interviewed said their unit staffing levels were inadequate. Staff said ensuring adequate staffing was particularly challenging when there were unplanned staff absences and they had to "scramble" to provide coverage. Some unit staff noted that this situation often resulted in units forcing nurses to work overtime or nurses floating to other units where they did not always have the qualifications to provide care. At some VAMCs, staff said there were increased staff injuries due to inadequate staffing. Furthermore, staff at one VAMC reported that where there had not been any changes made based on the unit staffing plans, their units continued to be understaffed to the detriment of both patient care and their job satisfaction.

VHA's Oversight to Ensure Its Nurse Staffing Methodology Is Implemented, Administered Appropriately, and Contributes to an Adequate and Qualified Nurse Workforce Is Limited

Our review of VHA's oversight of its nurse staffing methodology found that some internal controls—those related to environmental assessment, a plan for monitoring compliance, evaluation, timeliness of communication, and organizational accountability—are limited. The implementation of internal controls is necessary for ensuring initiatives achieve intended outcomes and for minimizing operational problems. Without these internal controls in place, VHA cannot ensure that its methodology meets department goals, such as establishing a standardized methodology for determining adequate and qualified nurse staffing at all VAMCs, and ultimately, having nurse staffing that is adequate to meet veterans' health care needs.

Environmental Assessment

VHA did not comprehensively assess each VAMC to ensure preparedness for implementing its methodology, including having the necessary technical support and resources, prior to the issuance of the methodology directive in 2010. Furthermore, as of August 2014, VHA did not have a plan for assessing whether VAMCs have the necessary resources to execute their approved nurse staffing plans. Under federal internal control standards, successful organizations monitor their internal and external environments continuously and systematically, and by building environmental assessments into the strategic planning process, are able to stay focused on long-term goals even as they make changes to achieve them.

VHA did not assess VAMCs' technical resources to determine if all VAMCs would be able to successfully implement the methodology. For example, the directive recommended that VAMCs use comparative data from external sources, such as the National Database of Nursing Quality Indicators (NDNQI) when analyzing unit-level staffing data. According to some VAMC officials, due to the costs and complexity of contracting,[33] not all VAMCs had access to this data source.[34] Each VAMC was responsible for establishing its own contract to purchase access to NDNQI data, which some VAMC officials said was expensive and time-consuming to set up, noting that it would have been helpful to have assistance in coordinating the contracting process. Officials from ONS reported that they are discussing the possibility of having a VHA-wide contract so that all VAMCs would have access to NDNQI data. In addition to access to comparative data, according to the directive, VAMCs need appropriate data system capabilities—in particular an automated staffing system for information such as patient admission, transfer and discharge data, and human resources data—to facilitate implementation of the data-driven methodology and calculation of NHPPD. However, not all VAMCs in our review had an automated staffing system in place even 3 years after the release of the directive. Officials at a VAMC without an automated staffing system told us staff were collecting and inputting data, in many cases manually, into a spreadsheet to calculate NHPPD, and that this process was extremely time-consuming and potentially error-prone. ONS officials said they knew VAMCs needed automated staffing systems when the directive was published in 2010. However, they thought Phase III—a national automated staffing system—would be forthcoming, and did not fully review whether VAMCs had alternative data capabilities to assist them in the interim.

When we asked how they assessed the readiness of VAMCs for implementation of the methodology, ONS officials told us that they did not do this as well as they should have for Phase I implementation in inpatient units, despite its 2009 Phase I pilot evaluation to better understand the potential capabilities and weaknesses of VAMCs. According to ONS, it still has not conducted such an assessment of all VAMCs even though it has moved forward with planning the national rollout of Phase II in operating room, emergency department, and spinal cord injury units. ONS, however, has assessed some of the available resources of the sites that have participated in the pilots for Phase II in spinal cord injury units. For example, ONS officials told us that they asked these participating sites questions about their access to data and nurse turnover within the pilot units to determine their ability to fully and successfully participate in the pilot. According to ONS officials, all sites reported that they were able to fully participate in the pilot. By not comprehensively assessing the VAMCs' technical support and resources to determine if they were prepared to implement the methodology, VHA had no assurance that the VAMCs would be successful.

Plan for Monitoring Compliance

ONS did not develop a plan for monitoring VAMCs to ensure they were in compliance with the implementation and ongoing administration of Phase I of the methodology. Under federal internal control standards, plans should be designed to ensure that ongoing monitoring occurs in the course of normal program operations, and managers should identify performance gaps in compliance with program policies and procedures.

ONS reported implementing two mechanisms for obtaining information from VAMCs—a 2013 questionnaire sent to all VAMCs and monthly methodology conference calls with VAMCs—but neither was an adequate mechanism for comprehensively assessing the compliance of each VAMC. The questionnaire, sent nearly 2 years after the deadline for implementation of Phase I of the methodology, asked VAMCs to report their status of staffing plan development, but because of lack of clarity in the questions asked, inconsistency in medical center responses, and lack of validation of the self-reported responses, it was not reliable for determining the extent to which VAMCs had developed staffing plans. ONS officials reported that they have no plans to survey VAMCs again on their status of developing staffing plans. Furthermore, the monthly methodology conference calls that started when the directive was published in 2010 did not provide an adequate mechanism for monitoring compliance because they too relied on VAMCs to self-report problems. A VAMC official told us that participants were reluctant to raise problems, such as not developing staffing plans on time, during these monthly calls.

In addition, the directive requires VAMCs to evaluate their staffing plans for Phase I annually, or more frequently if needed, but ONS officials told us that they did not have a systematic plan for monitoring compliance with this evaluation beyond the 2013 questionnaire and the monthly methodology conference calls. Moving forward, ONS officials said they plan to review whether all VAMCs implemented both the unit and facility expert panels, but, as of August 2014, had no detailed plan or timeline for conducting this review or for monitoring VAMCs' ongoing evaluation of their staffing plans. The lack of a plan for monitoring VAMCs' compliance with the implementation and ongoing administration of the methodology hinders VHA from being able to ensure that all VAMCs are staffing their nurses using the same, standardized methodology.

Evaluation

There have been limited evaluations of the methodology, and one of these evaluations has been significantly delayed. Under federal internal control standards, measuring performance allows organizations to track the progress they are making towards program goals and objectives, and provides managers important information on which to make management decisions and resolve any problems or program weaknesses.

- *Evaluation of Phase I pilot (conducted in September 2009)*—ONS identified VAMC challenges with implementing the methodology—such as difficulties accessing data, and staff nurses having an overall lack of knowledge of the methodology process. The evaluation contained recommendations, such as developing a training guidebook and providing guidelines on the role of the expert panels, to improve the methodology process. According to ONS, most of the recommendations from this 2009 evaluation have been addressed; however, we found that weaknesses identified in the 2009 evaluation still existed for all of the seven VAMCs included in our review.

- *Evaluations of Phase I national implementation and training (began early 2014, preliminary results were expected August 2014).* Similarly, ONS did not begin an evaluation of the national implementation of the methodology until January 2014, more than 2 years after VAMCs were required to have implemented it, and, as of August 2014, had still not been completed. According to ONS officials, the Phase I national evaluation was to review VAMCs' experiences during implementation, including a review of the training provided to VAMCs during that phase. The lengthy delay in the evaluation of Phase I was potentially problematic because the ongoing difficulties that VAMCs have experienced during implementation may have been avoided or resolved more quickly if the evaluation results had been available and corrective actions put into place. VAMC staff we interviewed told us they have been struggling with components of the methodology since the directive was issued. For example, some VAMC staff expressed difficulty completing and understanding the data analysis process for calculating NHPPD. An earlier evaluation of the methodology could have helped identify this problem, as well as potential solutions to address it. Furthermore, the delay limited ONS's time to apply lessons learned from Phase I evaluations to the implementation of Phase II, portions of which are already nearly complete.
- *Phase II pilot training evaluation (began in early 2014 with results expected November 2014)*—ONS is conducting an evaluation of the training that was provided to the VAMCs involved in the Phase II pilots in operating room, emergency department, and spinal cord injury units to determine if the training provided to these units needs to be changed in preparation for the national rollout. ONS officials told us that they have completed the operating room pilot; the national rollout of the methodology in operating room units in all VAMCs began in February 2014 and is expected to be completed by October 1, 2014. ONS officials said that it has completed the pilot for the emergency department units, but has not completed the pilot for spinal cord injury units; ONS has not scheduled deadlines for their national implementation.

VHA's delays in completing evaluations of the methodology limit its ability to identify and resolve VAMC implementation and administration problems, and thus help to ensure successful rollouts of subsequent phases of the methodology.

Timeliness of Implementation and Communication

The long timeline for implementing the pilots and national rollouts of Phases I and II, as well as evaluating Phase I of the staffing methodology—more than 7 years— and for communicating methodology-related information to VAMCs may have hindered the ability of VAMCs to develop their staffing plans and to execute the initiatives contained in those plans. Under federal internal control standards, timeliness in the development of a program or implementation of a policy is needed to maintain relevance and value in managing operations and making decisions. When information regarding a policy or program is not provided in a timely manner, there can be a loss of stakeholder support, which can affect how stakeholders make decisions. For example, staff from some VAMCs involved in the Phase II pilot stated that they believed the data and reports generated from the methodology were only a paper exercise because they had not gotten any feedback from ONS on next steps. ONS officials told us they have communicated information on the Phase II pilot, such as the status of the pilot and feedback obtained from the training sessions, through their monthly conference calls with VAMCs; however, based on our interviews, this information did not reach many staff at the VAMCs in our review that participated in the Phase II pilot.

Furthermore, ONS officials have not adequately communicated to VAMCs the status of Phase III of the methodology—development of a national automated staffing system. According to the directive, a national automated staffing system was to be developed to support VAMCs in the implementation of the methodology. Because this automated staffing system has yet to be developed as per the directive, officials from two VAMCs told us they bought their own systems, which helped to effectively administer the methodology. ONS officials told us at the time the directive was published in 2010, Phase III implementation was an aspirational goal. ONS officials said they had expected VHA data system teams to begin the process of developing a national automated system; however, it was not made a department goal, and is not currently on the list of projects under consideration for funding. Having a variety of staffing systems, and thus inconsistent data variables across VAMCs, inhibits ONS's ability to adequately evaluate the effectiveness of the staffing methodology. If an automated staffing system is eventually developed under Phase III, VAMCs likely will have to dismantle the staffing systems they have created and restructure their data analysis processes, which likely will be time-consuming and costly. VHA's long timelines for the implementation and communication of methodology-related information put stakeholder support of the methodology at risk and increase the potential for duplication of efforts.

Organizational Accountability

VHA did not define areas of responsibility or establish the appropriate line of reporting within the framework of VA's management structure for the ongoing administration and oversight of the methodology. Under federal internal control standards, an agency's organizational structure should provide management with a framework for planning, directing, and controlling operations to achieve agency objectives; a good internal control environment requires that the agency clearly defines key areas of authority and responsibility. VHA does not require VAMCs to submit any information or reports on the implementation and ongoing administration of the methodology to ONS or the VISNs. Such information, if it were shared, may have been used to inform ONS of any systematic problems that necessitate changes to help ensure the continued viability of its methodology, as well as identify any best practices that have been implemented by VAMCs across the country. ONS officials told us that they did not require the VAMCs to submit any such documentation to ONS, because they made a conscious decision to not "micro-manage" the local process of nurse staffing.

Furthermore, VHA has not sufficiently utilized the VISN-level management structure in the implementation or ongoing administration of the methodology. While the methodology directive described a role for the VISNs, that role was limited to ensuring that resources are available to VAMCs as they try to staff their units; the directive did not mention a role in the implementation or ongoing administration of the actual methodology. As a result, VISNs have not been consistently aware of problems experienced by VAMCs in their region, and have not provided support or education. In our interviews with VISN officials representing each of the seven VAMCs in our review, we found that three of the VISNs were not substantively involved in the implementation and ongoing administration of the methodology. According to ONS, in many VISNs, discussions of staffing methodology implementation were minimal, and rather than VISN leadership, the nurse executives, in addition to their responsibilities within their individual VAMCs, had the responsibility of disseminating staffing methodology-related information to the VAMCs within the VISN.

Staff from three VISNs that were more substantially involved in the implementation of the methodology provided oversight for the nurse staffing methodology and acted as liaisons for VAMC nurse executives for network-level issues. One VISN official we interviewed was developing oversight mechanisms for VAMCs in the region, including a requirement for nurse executives to submit a quarterly staffing report. According to the official, having such a reporting requirement at the VISN level would give the right amount of emphasis to the process and provide support to nurse executives implementing the methodology in the VAMCs. The quarterly report could also help inform VISN officials about issues with the methodology. This official was developing these mechanisms independently of ONS, but they could be considered potential best practices to be shared across all VISNs.

ONS officials told us they thought ideas or problems across VAMCs related to the methodology would be shared through the VAMC nurse executives. They also hoped that VISN leadership would be interested in the methodology and, as a result, schedule VISN-level briefings to aid in its implementation. VHA, however, did not specify either of these roles in the directive or take steps to ensure that they were occurring. Moving forward, ONS officials said they are considering developing a VISN-level staff position that would specifically focus on educating VAMCs within the region about the methodology, and assisting them with implementing it. Without clearly defined roles and responsibilities within VA's organizational structure, VHA's ability to improve its oversight of the implementation and administration of the staffing methodology and provide VAMCs with additional resources to assist with problems is compromised.

CONCLUSION

As the number of veterans requiring care in VAMCs and the complexity of services needed by many of these veterans increase, the need for an adequate and qualified nurse workforce is increasingly critical. Although VHA's nurse staffing methodology was intended to provide a nationally standardized methodology for determining and ensuring adequate and qualified nurse staffing at VAMCs, its ability to do so across all 151 VAMCs is not likely to be realized unless existing weaknesses are addressed. Although some improvements in nurse staffing were reported with the implementation of the staffing methodology, the seven VAMCs in our review experienced problems developing and executing the related staffing plans, including problems pertaining to data resources, training, and communication. Many of these problems persist as the seven VAMCs continue to administer the methodology.

We also found that VHA's oversight of the staffing methodology is limited and in many cases lacks sufficient internal controls, which could diminish VHA's ability to ensure an adequate and qualified nurse workforce. In particular, VHA has not adequately assessed the needs or preparedness of VAMCs to effectively implement the methodology, does not have a formal mechanism to ensure VAMCs' ongoing compliance with the methodology, has not clearly defined a role in oversight for VISNs, and does not regularly communicate with VAMCs or VISNs to cull and share best practices system-wide. Furthermore, delays in VHA's evaluations of early phases of the staffing methodology have made them too late to be useful in designing future phases or helping VAMCs with implementation. Because the implementation and administration of the nurse staffing methodology is ongoing, it is critical that VHA improve its oversight to help ensure an adequate and qualified nurse workforce across all VAMCs.

RECOMMENDATIONS FOR EXECUTIVE ACTION

To help ensure adequate and qualified nurse staffing at VAMCs, we recommend that the Secretary of Veterans Affairs direct the Interim Under Secretary for Health to enhance VHA's internal controls through the following five actions:

1) Provide support to all VAMCs to meet the objectives of the VHA directive, including:
    a) training that more clearly aligns with the needs of VAMC staff and
    b) a systematic process for collecting and disseminating staffing methodology best practices;
2) Conduct an environmental assessment of all VAMCs, including an assessment of their data analysis needs, to determine their preparedness to implement the remaining phases of the methodology, and use that information to help guide and provide the necessary

support for the implementation of the remaining phases and for the ongoing administration of the methodology;

3) Develop and implement a documented process to assess VAMCs' ongoing compliance with the staffing methodology, including assessing VAMCs' execution of staffing plans and more clearly defining the role and responsibilities of all organizational components, including VISNs, in the oversight and administration of the methodology;

4) Complete evaluations of Phase I and Phase II and make any necessary changes to policies and procedures before national implementation of Phase II in all VAMCs; and

5) Improve the timeliness and regularity of communication with VAMCs, including unit-level staff, regarding the status of the various phases of the methodology.

Agency Comments

We provided a draft of this report to VA for its review and comment. VA provided written comments. In its written comments, VA generally agreed with our conclusions and concurred with all five of the report's recommendations. To address the recommendations, VA indicated that VHA will take a number of actions, such as developing a written document specifying its process for assessing ongoing compliance with the staffing methodology and improving the timeliness and regularity of communication with VAMCs through face-to-face regional training sessions. VA indicated that target completion dates for implementing these recommendations range from September 2015 through September 2016. Regarding the recommendation that VA complete evaluations of Phase I and Phase II before national implementation of Phase II in all VAMCs, VA indicated that, by September 2016, it would complete its evaluations and determine what opportunities exist to modify policies and procedures, but did not explicitly state that the evaluations would be completed before national implementation. We continue to emphasize the importance of completing the evaluations before national implementation of Phase II in all VAMCs.

Sincerely yours,
Debra A. Draper
Director, Health Care

End Notes

[1] See, for example, R.L. Kane et al., *Nurse Staffing and Quality of Patient Care*, Pub. No. 07-E005, March 2007, Agency for Healthcare Research and Quality; and Kaiser Permanente Institute for Health Policy, *Nurse Staffing and Care Delivery Models: A Review of the Evidence* (Menlo Park, Calif.: March 2002).

[2] Pub. L. No. 107-135, Title I, § 124, 115 Stat. 2446, 2452 (Jan. 23, 2002).

[3] See Department of Veterans Affairs, Office of the Inspector General, *Healthcare Inspection: Evaluation of Nurse Staffing in Veterans Health Administration Facilities*, 03-00079-183 (Washington, D.C.: Aug. 13, 2004).

[4] See GAO, *VA Health Care: Improved Staffing Methods and Greater Availability of Alternate and Flexible Work Schedules Could Enhance the Recruitment and Retention of Inpatient Nurses*, GAO-09-17 (Washington, D.C.: Oct. 24, 2008).

[5] VA assigns each VAMC a complexity score derived from multiple variables to measure facility complexity arrayed along four categories, namely: patient population served, clinical services offered, education and research complexity, and administrative complexity.

[6] Magnet status is a designation of the Magnet Recognition Program®—a nationwide program developed by the American Nurses Credentialing Center, a subsidiary of the American Nurses Association, to recognize health care organizations for quality patient care, nursing excellence, and innovations in professional nursing practice. To attain Magnet status, hospitals must meet certain requirements, related to areas including staffing practices and quality monitoring.

[7] We spoke with officials from the Disabled American Veterans and Paralyzed Veterans of America who are knowledgeable about nurse staffing methodologies in VAMC inpatient units, such as spinal cord injury units.

[8] We interviewed officials from the American Nurses Association. We also contacted each of the nursing organizations that VHA officials told us work with VA nurses: American Federation of Government Employees, National Nurses United, National Association of Government Employees, National Federation of Federal Employees, and Nurses Organization of Veterans Affairs.

[9] Each of VA's 21 VISNs is responsible for managing and overseeing VAMCs within a defined geographic area.

[10] GAO, *Managing For Results: GPRA Modernization Act Implementation Provides Important Opportunities to Address Government Challenges*, GAO-11-617T (Washington, D.C.: May 10, 2011); *Executive Guide: Effectively Implementing the Government Performance and Results Act*, GAO/GGD-96-118 (Washington, D.C.: June 1996); *Standards for Internal Control in the Federal Government*, GAO/AIMD-00-21.3.1 (Washington, D.C.: November 1999); *Internal Control Management and Evaluation Tool*, GAO-01-1008G (Washington, D.C.: August 2001); *VA Dialysis Pilot: Increased Attention to Planning, Implementation, and Performance Measurement Needed to Help Achieve Goals*, GAO-12-584 (Washington, D.C.: May 23, 2012); *Managing For Results: Executive Branch Should More Fully Implement the GPRA Modernization Act to Address Pressing Governance Challenges*, GAO-13-518 (Washington, D.C.: June 26, 2013).

[11] According to VHA, the workforce data for RNs also include RNs with advanced degrees such as nurse practitioners.

[12] LPNs and licensed vocational nurses have the same level of education and patient care responsibilities. For the purposes of this report, when we refer to LPNs, we are referring to both LPNs and licensed vocational nurses.

[13] VHA also employs nurses to work outside VAMCs, such as those employed within its administrative offices. These nurses were not included in our review.

[14] See Department of Veterans Affairs, Veterans Health Administration, 2013 *Workforce Succession Strategic Plan* (Washington, D.C.: 2013).

[15] VHA's directive defines direct patient care as all patient- or resident-centered nursing activities performed by staff assigned to the unit. These activities include nursing assessments, admission and discharge activities, and patient teaching and communication.

[16] J. Spetz et al., "How Many Nurses Per Patient?" *Health Services Research*, vol. 43 (October 2008):1674-1692; Carayon, P. and A. Gurses, "Nursing Workload and Patient Safety in Intensive Care Units: A Human Factors Engineering Evaluation of the Literature," *Intensive and Critical Care Nursing*, vol. 21 (2005): 284-301; and American Association of Critical-Care Nurses, *Standards for Establishing and Sustaining Healthy Work Environments* (Aliso Viejo, Calif.: American Association of Critical-Care Nurses, 2005).

[17] According to ONS officials, the staffing methodology for these units were to be implemented separately from those included in Phase I because of the potential need to modify the methodology to align with the special services these units provide.

[18] See Department of Veterans Affairs, Office of the Inspector General, *Combined Assessment Program Summary Report: Evaluation of Nurse Staffing in Veterans Health Administration Facilities April – September 2013*, Report No. 14-01072-140 (Washington, D.C.: May 12, 2014).

[19] See Department of Veterans Affairs, Office of the Inspector General, *Combined Assessment Program Summary Report: Evaluation of Nurse Staffing in Veterans Health Administration Facilities*, Report No. 13-01744-187 (Washington, D.C.: April 30, 2013).

[20] Joint Commission on Accreditation of Healthcare Organizations, *Health Care at the Crossroads: Strategies for Addressing the Evolving Nursing Crisis* (Chicago, Ill.: Joint Commission on Accreditation of Healthcare Organizations, 2002).

[21] See American Nurses Association, *Principles for Nurse Staffing, Second Edition* (Silver Spring, Md.: American Nurses Association, 2012).

[22] Institute of Medicine, *The Future of Nursing: Leading Change, Advancing Health* (Washington, D.C.: The National Academies Press, 2011).

[23] See R.L. Kane et al., *Nurse Staffing and Quality of Patient Care*, Pub. No. 07-E005, March 2007, Agency for Healthcare Research and Quality; and "Hospital Nurse Staffing and Quality of Care," *Agency for Healthcare Research and Quality, Research in Action*, Issue 14, Pub. No. 04-0029 (Rockville, Md.: 2004).

[24] M.A. Blegen et al., "Nurse Staffing Effects on Patient Outcomes: Safety-Net and NonSafety-Net Hospitals," *Medical Care*, vol. 49, issue 2 (April 2011), 406–414; J. Needleman et al., "Nurse Staffing and Inpatient Hospital Mortality," *New England Journal of Medicine*, vol. 364, issue 11 (March 2011), 1037-1045; L.H. Aiken et al., "Implications of the California Nurse Staffing Mandate for Other States," *Health Services Research*, vol. 45, issue 4 (April 2010), 904–921; and P.W. Stone et al., "Nurse Working Conditions and Patient Safety Outcomes," *Medical Care*, vol. 45, issue 6 (June 2007), 571-578.

[25] A.P. Bartel et al., "Human Capital and Productivity in a Team Environment: Evidence from the Healthcare Sector," *American Economic Journal: Applied Economics*, vol. 6, issue 2 (2014), 231-259.

[26] A. Kutney-Lee, D.M. Sloane, and L.H. Aiken, "An Increase In The Number Of Nurses with Baccalaureate Degrees Is Linked To Lower Rates Of Postsurgery Mortality," *Health Affairs*, vol. 32, issue. 3 (March 2013), 579-586; L.H. Aiken et al., "Effects of Hospital Care Environment on Patient Mortality and Nurse Outcomes," *Journal of Nursing*

Administration, vol. 38, issue 5 (May 2008), 223-229; and C.R. Friese et al., "Hospital Nurse Practice Environments and Outcomes for Surgical Oncology Patients," *Health Services Research*, vol. 43, issue 4 (August 2008), 1145-1163.

[27] J. Spetz, "Nurse Satisfaction and the Implementation of Minimum Nurse Staffing Regulations," *Policy, Politics, & Nursing Practice*, vol. 9 (Feb. 2008, first published on April 3, 2008), 15-21; and L.H. Aiken et al., "Hospital Nurse Staffing and Patient Mortality, Nurse Burnout, and Job Dissatisfaction," *The Journal of the American Medical Association*, vol. 288, issue 16 (October 2002), 1987-1993.

[28] A.W. Stimpfel, D.M. Sloane, and L.H. Aiken, "The Longer the Shifts for Hospital Nurses, the Higher the Levels of Burnout and Patient Dissatisfaction," *Health Affairs*, vol. 31, issue 11 (November 2012), 2501-2509; J.P. Cimiotti et al., "Nurse Staffing, Burnout, and Health Care-Associated Infection," *American Journal of Infection Control*, vol. 40 (August 2012) 486-490; and D.C. Vahey et al., "Nurse Burnout and Patient Satisfaction," *Medical Care*, vol. 42, issue 2 (Feb. 2004), 57-66.

[29] Fixed nurse-to-patient ratios assign a certain number of patients to each nurse (e.g., one nurse for every five patients) while adjustable, unit-specific, minimum staffing levels assign minimum ratios of nurses to patients for each unit and shift that reflects the needs of the patient population and matches the skills and experience of the staff.

[30] These are illustrative examples of different approaches; we did not conduct a comprehensive review of all state requirements.

[31] As previously described, VAMCs were required to implement the methodology in inpatient units (Phase I) no later than September 30, 2011. VAMCs were expected to implement the methodology in their operating rooms by October 1, 2014; requirements for implementation of Phase II in other units and Phase III of the methodology have not been set.

[32] Transport teams are staff who assist in transporting patients to and from appointments off the unit. Sitters are staff who provide one-on-one direct patient observation.

[33] NDNQI was created as part of the American Nurses Association's Patient Safety and Quality Initiative to identify the linkages between staffing and patient outcomes. The database contains data on quality indicators and staff levels collected from approximately 2,000 hospitals that submit data on nursing-sensitive indicators, such as pressure ulcers and patient falls. According to the American Nurses Association, 98 percent of all Magnet facilities use some aspect of NDNQI data.

[34] According to the staffing methodology directive, a comparative analysis of NHPPD data from other resources is also recommended, such as from the Labor Management Institute and NDNQI. Labor Management Institute data compare direct, indirect, and total worked hours of care by hospital and unit type, and NDNQI data contain information on quality indicators and staff levels.

INDEX

A

access, 18, 24, 52, 53
accountability, 33, 51
accreditation, 12
administrative support, 2, 17, 23, 24
advancement, 10
advancements, 14, 30
Afghanistan, 34
age, 7
aging population, 7
appointments, 32, 45, 63
assessment, 22, 33, 51, 53, 59
audit, 6, 36
authority, 57

B

barriers, 21
benefits, 2, 11, 12, 13, 16, 28
blood, 9, 38
blood pressure, 9, 38
bonuses, 18
burnout, 43

C

campaigns, 11
candidates, 11, 30
certification, 8
chain of command, 49
challenges, vii, 1, 2, 11, 17, 18, 19, 23, 24, 49, 54
Chicago, 62
clarity, 53
collaboration, 12, 13
colleges, 9, 38
color, iv
communication, 6, 32, 46, 48, 57, 60
community, 9, 18, 38, 49
comparative analysis, 63
competition, 2, 17, 23, 24
complexity, 6, 29, 35, 48, 52, 58, 61
compliance, 2, 6, 19, 20, 21, 24, 25, 32, 33, 51, 53, 54, 59, 60
computer, 47
conference, 53, 54, 56
Congress, iv, 4, 23, 34
consulting, 19
coordination, 23
cost, 18
cost of living, 18
credentials, 27, 30
curricula, 15
curriculum, 12, 15

D

damages, iv

data analysis, 47, 55, 57, 59
data collection, 21
database, 63
deaths, 4
Department of Health and Human Services, 29
depth, 41
directives, 6, 36
directors, 12, 13, 42
discharges, 8, 38, 41, 47
dissatisfaction, 2, 17, 18
draft, 25, 60

E

education, 2, 4, 8, 9, 12, 13, 14, 16, 27, 28, 29, 30, 38, 57, 61
emergency, 18, 35, 42, 53, 55
employees, 13, 15, 16, 17, 22
employment, 10, 12, 15, 18, 45
environment, 36, 57
environments, 22
equipment, 8, 38
evidence, 6, 36
execution, 32, 35, 42, 44, 48, 60
exercise, 56
expenditures, 12
expertise, 18, 47
external environment, 52

F

federal government, 30
Federal Government, 29, 61
financial, 2, 12, 13, 15, 18, 19, 23, 47
financial incentives, 13, 18, 23
financial resources, 47
fiscal year, 3, 5, 9, 10, 15, 28, 33, 34
funding, 5, 12, 13, 18, 19, 20, 22, 28, 56
funds, 12, 13, 18

G

GAO, vii, 1, 2, 4, 6, 9, 10, 14, 16, 26, 27, 28, 29, 30, 31, 32, 36, 38, 39, 40, 45, 46, 61
governance, 41, 49, 51
GPRA, 3, 6, 29, 61
graduate education, 13
graduate students, 13
growth, 4
guidance, 6, 11, 20, 24, 36
guidelines, 35, 38, 54

H

health, 3, 7, 9, 23, 24, 30, 33, 37, 38, 43, 51, 61
health care, 3, 7, 9, 23, 24, 30, 33, 37, 43, 51, 61
health care system, 7
high school, 9, 38
high school diploma, 9, 38
hiring, 11, 12, 13, 19, 49, 50
House, 4, 34
House of Representatives, 4, 34
human, 3, 11, 17, 22, 42, 47, 52
human resources, 3, 11, 17, 22, 47, 52
hygiene, 9

I

improvements, 2, 5, 25, 32, 50, 59
increased competition, vii, 1, 4
individuals, 41
injuries, 51
injury, iv, 53, 55
intensive care unit, 4, 8, 18, 37
internal controls, 6, 32, 33, 36, 51, 59
Iraq, 34
issues, 18, 24, 35, 58

J

job satisfaction, 37, 43, 50, 51
justification, 15

L

laws, 19
laws and regulations, 19
leadership, 18, 20, 23, 48, 57, 58
learning, 12, 22, 48
legislation, 34, 43
level of education, 8, 38, 61

M

management, 3, 21, 23, 24, 29, 32, 33, 41, 54, 57
marketing, 11
matter, iv
medical, vii, 1, 2, 4, 5, 6, 7, 8, 9, 11, 12, 13, 14, 15, 16, 17, 18, 19, 20, 21, 22, 23, 24, 25, 26, 28, 29, 30, 32, 34, 37, 38, 43, 53
medical care, 34
medication, 43
mental health, 8, 18, 50
methodology, vii, 31, 32, 33, 35, 36, 37, 38, 41, 42, 44, 47, 48, 49, 51, 52, 53, 54, 55, 56, 57, 58, 59, 60, 62, 63
military, 34
mission, 4, 7, 22, 24
missions, 29
Montana, 35
mortality, 43
mortality rate, 43

N

national policy, 35
New England, 62
North America, 29
nurses, vii, 1, 2, 4, 5, 6, 7, 9, 10, 11, 12, 13, 14, 15, 16, 17, 18, 21, 22, 23, 24, 25, 26, 27, 28, 29, 30, 32, 34, 35, 37, 38, 41, 43, 44, 45, 48, 49, 50, 51, 54, 61, 62, 63
nursing, 3, 4, 5, 8, 9, 11, 12, 13, 14, 15, 18, 20, 22, 29, 30, 32, 33, 34, 35, 37, 38, 41, 43, 45, 47, 48, 50, 61, 62, 63
nursing care, 34, 51

O

Office of the Inspector General, 61, 62
officials, 1, 5, 6, 15, 17, 18, 19, 20, 21, 22, 23, 30, 31, 35, 36, 44, 47, 48, 49, 50, 52, 53, 54, 55, 56, 57, 58, 61, 62
Oklahoma, 5
on-the-job training, 12
operations, 19, 34, 53, 56, 57
opportunities, 10, 12, 13, 60
outpatient, 8, 18, 37
oversight, 2, 6, 20, 23, 24, 32, 33, 35, 36, 51, 57, 58, 59, 60
overtime, 51

P

participants, 15, 28, 54
patient care, 4, 7, 9, 26, 29, 35, 37, 38, 41, 43, 44, 45, 47, 48, 50, 51, 61, 62
permission, iv
personal hygiene, 38
physicians, 7, 29
pipeline, 23
pneumonia, 43
policy, 3, 24, 30, 34, 56
population, 7, 24, 29, 61, 63
preparation, iv, 55
preparedness, 33, 52, 59
principles, 41
private sector, 2, 17, 24
professionals, 13

Q

qualifications, 31, 32, 43, 50, 51
questionnaire, 53, 54

R

recommendations, iv, 2, 25, 32, 41, 54, 60
recruiting, 4, 5, 6, 11, 17, 18, 22, 37
regulations, 43
relevance, 56
reliability, 5
requirement, 20, 21, 58
requirements, 6, 8, 9, 12, 19, 20, 30, 37, 38, 61, 63
researchers, 36
resources, 2, 3, 21, 22, 23, 24, 25, 32, 33, 45, 46, 47, 52, 53, 57, 58, 59, 63
response, 2, 20
retirement, 10, 23, 27, 29, 37
rights, iv
risk, 43, 57
rural areas, 18

S

safety, 43
scholarship, 13, 14
school, 12, 13, 14, 15, 20, 38
scope, 9
service organization, 6, 29, 32, 36
service organizations, 6, 29, 32, 36
services, iv, vii, 1, 7, 8, 9, 10, 11, 20, 23, 24, 26, 29, 37, 38, 58, 61, 62
shortage, 29
signs, 9, 38
spending, 28
spinal cord, 35, 42, 53, 55, 61
spinal cord injury, 35, 42, 53, 55, 61
Spring, 62
staffing, vii, 5, 7, 8, 29, 31, 32, 33, 34, 35, 36, 37, 38, 41, 42, 43, 44, 45, 46, 47, 48, 49, 50, 51, 52, 53, 54, 56, 57, 58, 59, 60, 61, 62, 63
stakeholders, 4, 24, 25, 41, 56
state, 8, 9, 38, 60, 63
states, 43
statutory authority, 9, 30
strategic planning, 36, 52
structure, 32, 33, 57, 58
student enrollment, 12, 13
support services, 32, 41, 50
support staff, 4

T

target, 60
teams, 56, 63
technical support, 33, 52, 53
techniques, 47
time frame, 24
Title I, 61
tracks, 3
training, 2, 3, 8, 9, 12, 14, 15, 16, 18, 19, 21, 22, 23, 24, 25, 27, 32, 38, 46, 47, 50, 54, 55, 56, 59, 60
training programs, 22
transport, 41
treatment, 8, 38, 47
turnover, 1, 6, 10, 18, 22, 27, 29, 30, 35, 37, 43, 53

U

unions, 6, 29, 32
unit plan, 42
United States, v, vii, 1, 31
urban, 6, 35

V

vacancies, 9, 16, 49
validation, 53
variables, 29, 56, 61
variations, 14

W

wages, 28
Washington, 29, 30, 61, 62
well-being, 7

workforce, vii, 1, 2, 3, 4, 5, 7, 9, 10, 11, 21, 23, 24, 26, 30, 31, 33, 35, 36, 37, 41, 58, 59, 61

working conditions, 43
workplace, 43